# NORTHUMBERLAND

*a photographer's view*

# NORTHUMBERLAND

## *a photographer's view*

*photographed by* KEITH ALLARDYCE

*foreword by* MAGNUS MAGNUSSON

ISBN: 0-9513339-0-9
British Library Cataloguing-in-Publication Data
Published by The Viewfinder Press 1992

*Designed by* Susan Harvey Design©
*Printed in Great Britain by* Chatsworth Studios

When I think of Northumberland, I think of frontier country, of land that has long been under siege but is still unsubdued. Mountain and moorland, cliffs and coastline, sturdy towns and country hamlets and solid greystone villages shouldering the wind: that is the land "North of the Humber".

It has always been a land for pioneers pitting themselves against the elements and each other. It was the No Man's Land north of Hadrian's Wall, as the Romans sought to consolidate the north-western limits of Empire. It was castle country and tower country, the uneasy domain of strongholds with hard minatory names like Bamburgh and Dunstanburgh and Kielder and Warkworth. It was essentially Border country, where the English pushed a mailed fist north of the Tweed to hold Berwick like a knuckleduster, where Carter Bar offers a dramatic view of the Scottish Lowlands after the travail of the Cheviots and where the Lords of Redesdale strove to impose their own arbitrary writ on the lawlessness of frontier life.

But it was a land for pioneers of the spirit, too, where Lindisfarne, the Holy Island, provided a haven on the way to heaven for the apostles of a more enduring writ. On that hallowed demi-isle, missionary saints like Aidan and Cuthbert created a mother church of Celtic Christianity for the north, a seminary of the soul whose graduates would spread the word far afield over Britain and the Continent.

The profile of a place is also the profile of the people who inhabit it. The natural facets of Northumberland are reflected in the faces of the men and women and children who commit their lives and labour to taming the rough land and the restless sea that pounds its bulwarks.

It is essentially through them, the people of Northumberland, that this telling portrait of England's frontier country is evoked. Keith Allardyce is himself a Northumbrian, a natural frontiersman who loves to patrol the boundaries of habitation. This book is his salute.

*Magnus Magnusson*

## ACKNOWLEDGEMENTS

My sincere thanks go to all those people in Northumberland who helped me in many ways during the photography and production of this book.

My special thanks go to George Stephenson, Director of MidNAG, for two commissions to photograph in Northumberland and for financial support towards publishing costs, to the Countryside Commission for a joint commission with MidNAG to photograph farming in Northumberland, to Magnus Magnusson for his foreword, and to Susan Harvey for the design of this book.

Mid NAG

## MINI-BIOGRAPHY

Keith Allardyce is the professional name of photographer Keith Hobbs. Born in Ashington, Northumberland, he studied at Harrow School of Photography before becoming a medical photographer in a teaching hospital, and a departmental photographer at Imperial College, London. He has been an RSPB summer warden in Orkney, spent two years in a Steiner community, and was a photographer for Hadrian's Wall Museums. He is now a free-lance photographer specialising in book illustration.

His interest in Scotland led him to become a roving relief lighthouse keeper for one year, and later a keeper stationed at Sule Skerry Lighthouse over thirty miles west of Orkney, for almost two years. These experiences led to his first book 'At Scotland's Edge', containing over 170 photographs on the life of the lighthouse keepers of Scotland and the Isle of Man.

## DEDICATION

For Mum and Dad
Win and Jim Hobbs of Ashington

Northumberland is a place of wide plains, which sweep from bright sandy bays and stark headlands braced against the North Sea, to high moorland borders with Scotland and Cumbria. To the south lie Newcastle and Tyneside's spreading conurbation, and the wild Durham hills.

Northumberland is a place apart, remaining independent by nature, like Cornwall and Yorkshire, and retains an individuality in a world which moves increasingly towards uniformity.

This area is a remnant of Northumbria, a Kingdom which extended, over a thousand years ago, from the Humber to the Forth. The Tweed was then at its centre. Today, the county of Northumberland is the fifth largest and the most northerly in England. It spans an area of almost two thousand square miles and is mainly agricultural, with its industrial region confined to the south-east corner where half of the county's 300,000 people live.

The English Tourist Board has called Northumberland "England's best kept secret", as it has escaped the attentions of mass tourism, unlike its spectacular neighbour to the west, the Lake District. Many travellers simply pass through Northumberland, gaining only a glimpse of the place without a hint of its secrets, from the Great North Road, the A1, or through the carriage windows of the London to Edinburgh express.

The coast of Northumberland extends from Seaton Sluice in the south, on the border with Tyne and Wear, to a farm called Marshall Meadows three miles north of Berwick upon Tweed. In almost every sheltered bay along its length there are villages and hamlets each with its fishing cobles, high-prowed and blunt-sterned; these boats, with their curvaceous Norse style and gaudy colours, are usually given beautiful and romantic names by their hardy owners.

During the summer months it is mostly for salmon that the fishermen cast their nets into the North Sea. (There are fixed nets at Goswick Sands, just north of Holy Island, and at Tweedmouth men still row out into the estuary to encircle salmon with a net let out behind a small, flat-bottomed boat, before hauling the net from the shore.)

In September when the salmon season ends, and throughout the winter, the inshore fishermen set pots for lobsters and crabs. Though the herring fleets have disappeared long ago from this coast, herring, landed now on Scotland's north-east coast, are still taken to Craster's kipper sheds where fish have been cured in oak smoke since the thirteenth century.

Wildlife abounds along the coast; grey seals and common seals, so often at odds with the fishermen, breed on the Farne Islands where the Great Whin Sill, a dolerite ridge which extends diagonally across the county, emerges between one and a half and five miles off-shore. These islands are the breeding grounds, too, of vast colonies of sea-birds, and each summer thousands of visitors sail from Seahouses, a curious village of amusement arcades and chip shops, to look at the spectacle. Part of the experience is seeing the 'Pinnacles', tall black rocks, crowded with guillemots, and being stabbed by fierce terns, and walking within inches of eider ducks sitting tight on their nests.

The islands are probably the world's first bird sanctuary, through Cuthbert, the shepherd who became Bishop of Lindisfarne and Northumberland's most-loved saint; Cuthbert lived on the islands briefly, in solitude and in the contemplation of God. Even today eiders are known locally as Cuddy's ducks after this extraordinary holy man. Cuthbert died in 687 AD in his tiny prayer cell on the Inner Farne after a short illness.

The Farne Islands were also the home of the heroine, Grace Darling. With her father, the light-keeper of the Longstone Lighthouse in the Outer Farnes, she rescued the survivors of the wrecked steamer the 'Forfarshire', from the Big Harcar Rock half a mile from the lighthouse, on a windy September morning in 1838.

Almost six miles up the coast from the Farnes lies Holy Island, for centuries known as Lindisfarne. It is accessible at low tide, when a causeway is uncovered across the vast expanse of mud-flats between the island and the mainland. The village of Holy Island has a population of about 200 people, and flourishes on fishing and tourism.

It was on Holy Island that St Aidan founded a monastery, having travelled from Iona, Scotland's holy island, to establish Christianity in King Oswald's Kingdom of Northumbria in the early seventh century; and it was on Holy Island that Cuthbert's body was initially buried, soon after he died in his Farne Island cell.

In Cuthbert's honour, during the 690's, the magnificent Lindisfarne Gospels were produced in Lindisfarne's monastery. These priceless treasures, a text from the four

Gospels, are written in fine script with beautiful illustrations on 258 sheets of vellum. They were produced by one man, a dedicated and talented monk, Eadfrith, and are now held in the British Library, London.

Since Cuthbert's death there has been an annual pilgrimage of Christians to Holy Island, this cradle of English Christianity (though Cuthbert's remains have lain in the high altar of Durham Cathedral since 1104).

In contrast to the breath-taking, timeless northern shores of Northumberland, the coast at Lynemouth, some fourteen miles north of the Tyne, suffers severely from the effects of industry. Here British Coal have dumped waste material from the nearby Ellington mine for many years. The comparatively small amount of coal within the waste is washed ashore, where the black tide has created a black beach almost two miles long. But this 'waste' provides a living for a band of people, sea-coalers, who live in caravans just above the shore. They collect the coal when the tide and wind are suitable, and sell it to neighbouring house-holders.

The Ellington mine is the last to be worked by British Coal in the Northumberland coal field. The coal-face is now over seven miles out under the sea, and surprisingly pit-ponies are used in the mine, the last pit-ponies in Britain. Around two million tons of coal are mined here each year, a production output which has frequently broken all European records. Much of the coal is for export, while some is used by Blyth Power Station, and by the neighbouring Alcan Power Station which serves Alcan's aluminium smelter. Alcan produce one-third of Britain's aluminium at their Lynemouth smelter. Its raw material, bauxite, is delivered by ship to Blyth where it is transferred to rail for delivery to the smelter.

The industrial part of the coast ends abruptly at Lynemouth, and beyond lies Druridge Bay, almost six miles of golden sand backed by high dunes. The remnants of World War II here lend an air of drama to the place: there are rows of anti-tank blocks above the beach. But this precious landscape is under threat. The Central Electricity Generating Board have ear-marked Druridge as a possible site for a nuclear power station. There is almost total opposition to the plan in the north-east of England, where coal has for years been the traditional source of power. The appalling history of radiation leaks and 'cover-ups' at the Windscale Power Station (given a fresh new name, Sellafield), less than 100 miles away on the Cumbrian coast, has bred total mistrust of the nuclear industry in many Northumbrians.

History is never far away in Northumberland. There are more castles here than anywhere else in Britain, and many are vast, imposing buildings built to protect this once turbulent border. The countryside is also dotted with pele towers which once provided protection for the people and their livestock during the days of the border reivers, when sheep stealing and cattle rustling by both the Scots and the Northumbrians, was a way of life.

The first Viking raids towards the end of the eighth century brought devastation and terror to these shores, and a second invasion by the Danish warriors a century later, attacking from the south, destroyed almost everything in their path between the Tyne and the Tweed. The Vikings did settle here too for a while, but they left few place names in their wake. Lucker, near Belford, is almost the only example to be found.

Near the village of Branxton in north Northumberland is the site of the bloodiest battle ever fought on this border. It is the site of the Battle of Flodden Field, the most tragic of all the battles between the English and the Scots. If you stand by its memorial stone, inscribed simply "To the Brave of both Nations", and look across the large, rolling fields which now make a patchwork over the battle ground, you can still feel the great sadness of that terrible day, September 9th, 1513. Flodden was a major battle with far-reaching consequences all over Europe; when the battle was over, King James IV of Scotland lay dead, and with him most of his nobility and soldiers, in total over 10,000 men. Of the English, at least 1,500 men were slaughtered. The tragedy will always be remembered in the haunting lament, played on the pipes, 'The Flowers of the Forest'.

The most extraordinary historical feature in the county must be the Roman Wall, which extends across England from the Tyne to the Solway; it marks the north British limit of Hadrian's empire, and has towns, camps and forts along its entire length. The wall is now much lower than its original height, since weathering, and the removal of stones for houses and farm buildings which went on for centuries, took their toll. It is possible that originally the wall was white, gleaming with a layer of lime mortar, which would have given the defences a more threatening appearance to the northern enemies, the Scots and Picts.

The best place to see the Wall is along the rough sheep country above the River South Tyne near Sewing Shields, Twice Brewed and Cawfields. Some of the Roman treasures, in metal, stone, pottery and glass, found by archaeologists near the Wall, can be seen in the museums at Chesters, Housesteads and Vindolanda.

Here and there throughout the landscape are standing stones, traces of small stone circles, and stones with strange carvings, peculiar to Northumberland, known as cup and ring marks. These are traces of some of the earliest people, who still remain a mystery to us. And an earlier race, probably the first to settle in the region, are the 'pigmy flint' people, named after their flint weapons: tiny arrow heads and spear tips. Their last refuge in Northumberland was the Farne Islands, surviving there until shortly before Cuthbert's time.

Across the industrial corner of the county, where the Northumberland coal-field prospered during the 19th and 20th centuries, the past is being swept away under a wave of industrial estates and housing estates.

With the exception of Ellington, the collieries which once flourished here, with pit heaps like little Fujiamas standing by their compact pit villages, have vanished. The pit heaps have been completely removed, or at least rounded-off and disguised with trees or turf. The character of the place has changed completely with the mine closures, and the housing estates which spread over and around the once neat and self-contained communities all end up looking alike, and no different from, say, the estates around Chelmsford in Essex.

From well over 100 collieries in its hey-day, Northumberland has only one coal-mine left. The last pit but one was at Ashington, where the world's biggest mining village developed after the mine's opening in the 1860s. Ashington has some of the longest terraced housing in Europe, named 7th Row, 8th Row and 9th Row, and others named after heroines from Shakespeare, and trees. The town is famous for its football families, the Charltons and Milburns, and for its top international opera singers, Sheila Armstrong and Janice Cairns.

Ashington is also well known in the art world for a group of miners who started a painting class in 1934 under the Workers' Educational Programme. These artists are known as the 'Ashington Group' who studied together in an experiment of 'seeing by doing.' The Group's last surviving founder-member, Oliver Kilbourn, has won acclaim for his remarkable collection of paintings on the theme 'My Life as a Pitman'.

Since the recent closure of Woodhorn Colliery, near Ashington,the buildings have been turned into a mining museum, as a monument to north-east miners. There are other monuments to miners, if you look carefully. At New Hartley, between the back gardens of two rows of houses, there is the capped entrance to the mine where, in 1834, 204 men and boys died underground. They died slowly through suffocation following the collapse of the engine-beam in the mine's only entrance shaft. In Earsdon church-yard, amongst old sycamores and ivy, stands their tall monument on which is inscribed 'Be not deceived; God is not mocked: for whatsoever a man soweth, that he will also reap'.

There have been many colliery closures by British Coal, the cause of the 1984/85 miners' strike which brought great bitterness and division in the close mining communities. But there has also been the development of large-scale coal excavation in Northumberland by the Open Cast Coal Executive. Their method is to create vast quarries by removing millions of tons of shale to reach the coal seams. An army of men, cranes and lorries is involved in these operations, and at Butterwell, near Morpeth, the biggest mobile crane in the world, 'Big Geordie', can scoop 100 tons of material at a time with its mammoth clawed bucket.

Elsewhere in Northumberland purpose-built industrial estates provide facilities for a vast range of small businesses, from growing mushrooms to manufacturing industrial tools. There is even a new business which breeds lug-worms, using Alcan's waste hot water from its power station, to provide bait for the sea-angling market. Next to Blyth Power Station, a small business makes heat-insulation materials using some of the furnace ash from the station.

There are much larger businesses and industries, such as Bedlington's Welwyn Electric, making components for the world's electronic needs; Boots, Searle, and Merck, Sharp and Dohme, manufacturing drugs; Lonrho Textiles; and Wilkinson Sword.

The whole of Northumberland is tilted towards the North Sea; it is dissected by a series of beautiful rivers, all of which except the South Tyne have their source in the

Cheviot Hills. This is principally farming country. The main market towns in the countryside are Morpeth, Alnwick, Hexham, Bellingham, Rothbury and Wooler, and there is a host of rural villages dependent entirely on the agricultural economy.

Seventy per cent of the land is used for grazing livestock, mostly sheep and cattle, and each week animals are auctioned at the local marts. The uplands of Northumberland act as a kind of reservoir, providing lambs for fattening on the farms in the county's more lush, lowland areas. Cattle, both beef and dairy, thrive on the lowland farms too; and there are now, increasingly, experiments in alternative land uses, such as rearing goat herds for their milk, hair, hide and meat, and even milking sheep for cheese production, and catering for tourists.

Over 20% of the agriculture's acreage is used for growing cereals, but it is a decreasing acreage due to demands on farmers to reduce the present over-production.

Some farmers are beginning to plant trees, particularly deciduous trees, as part of alternative land-use policy. There is certainly a shortage of large, mature deciduous trees, but they can be found in small pockets especially around some of the large estates such as those of the Duke of Northumberland, Lord Joicey and Lord Allendale.

Trees of a different nature blanket vast areas around Kielder and Wark. These are the pine forests of the Forestry Commission, planted initially immediately following the First World War in a scheme to overcome Britain's serious timber shortages. Kielder Forest is Europe's largest man-made forest, which now contains Europe's largest man-made reservoir, Kielder Water, opened in 1982 by the Northumbrian Water Authority. Many farms were drowned forever when the reservoir filled, just as many farms and moorland grazing were smothered when the Forestry Commission marched over their land.

There is a living link with ancient Britain at Chillingham, near Wooler, where a 5O-strong herd of wild white cattle roam on the Countess of Tankerville's estate. These large, long-horned animals are decendants of our native cattle, and are frequently used for scientific study; one of their peculiarities is that they do not not suffer from constant in-breeding.

In a landscape which is continuously changing, with land-use becoming increasingly mechanised, the farming communities still attach great importance to the agricultural shows which are held throughout the summer. You will see at any show people taking great pride in the appearance of their livestock, lovingly grooming the animals' coats, and presenting magnificent examples of vegetables and flowers for display and competition.

The agricultural shows celebrate the farmers' life on the land; and they remind us, like the harvest festivals, of our need to be close to the earth; and each October at Alwinton, in the magnificent setting of Upper Coquetdale, the farmers hold the last show of the year in the county, the 'land of far horizons'.

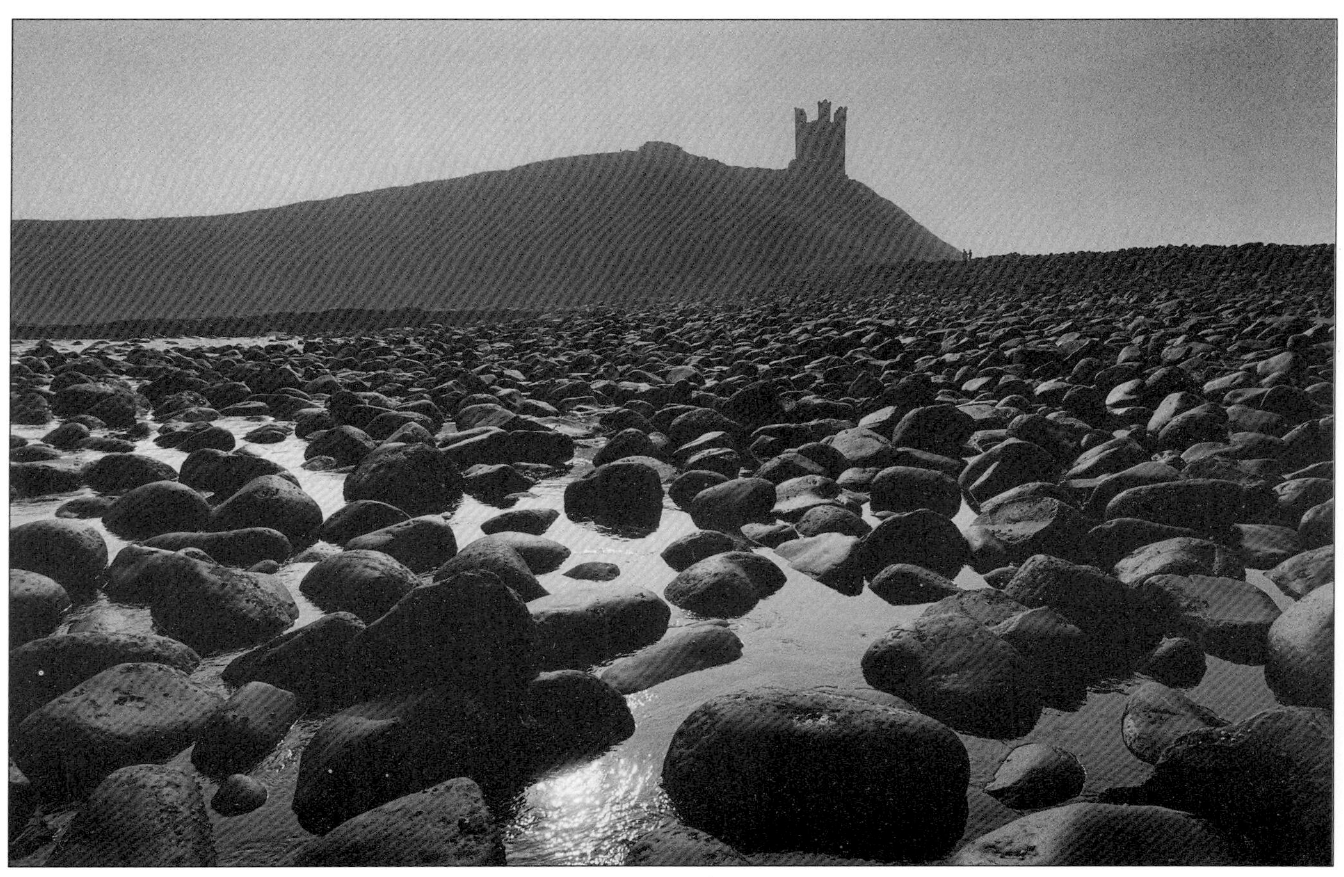

*Lilburn Tower, Dunstanburgh Castle*

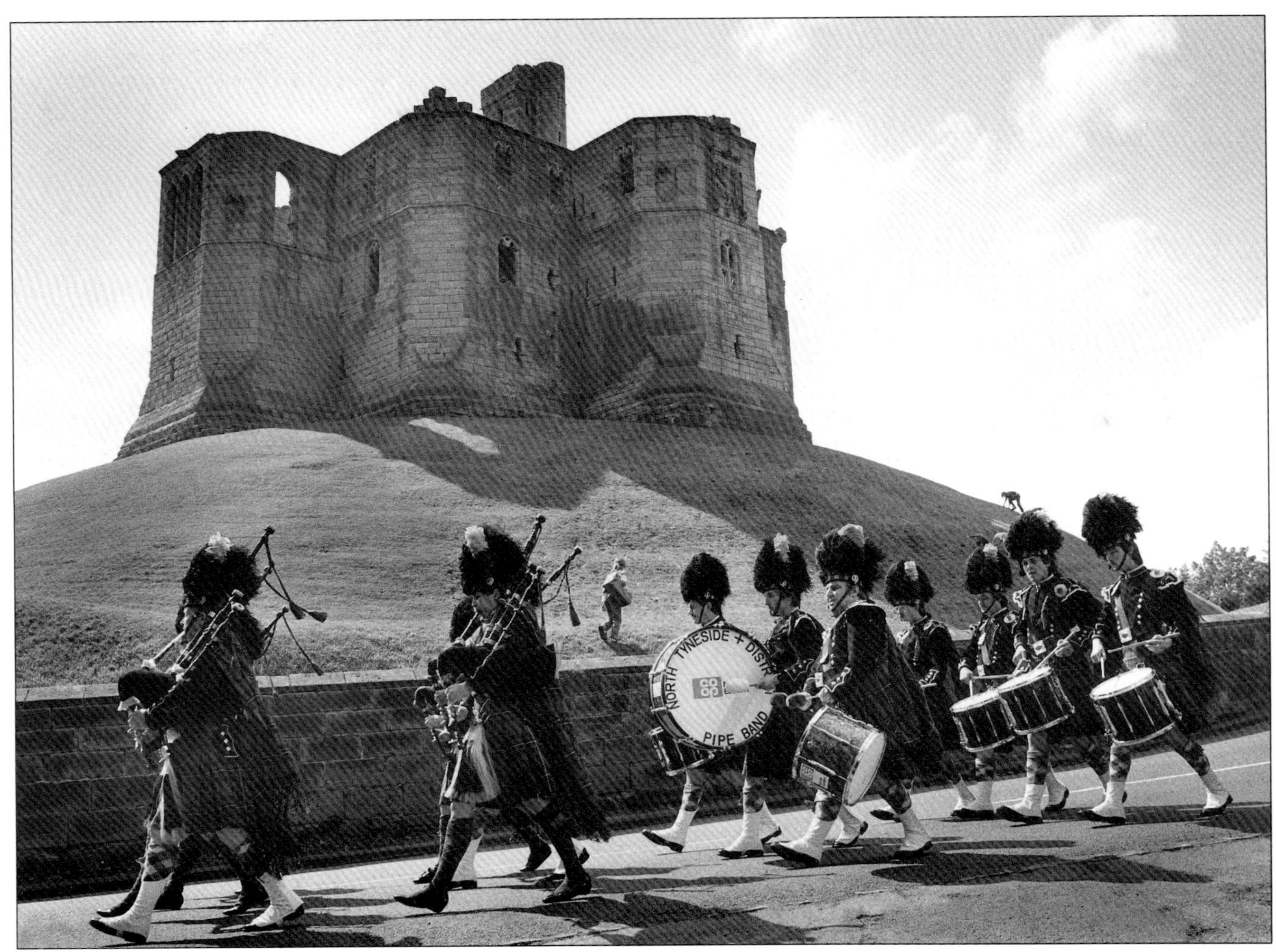


*Marching to Warkworth Flower Show*

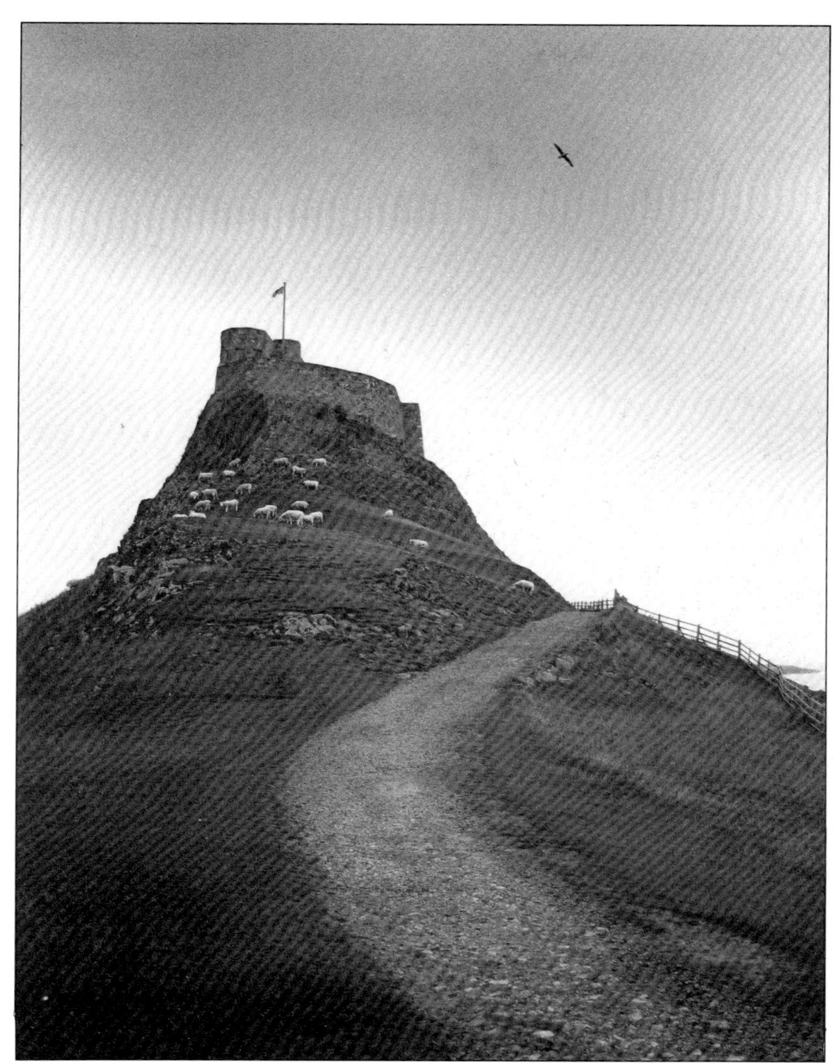

*Holy Island Castle*

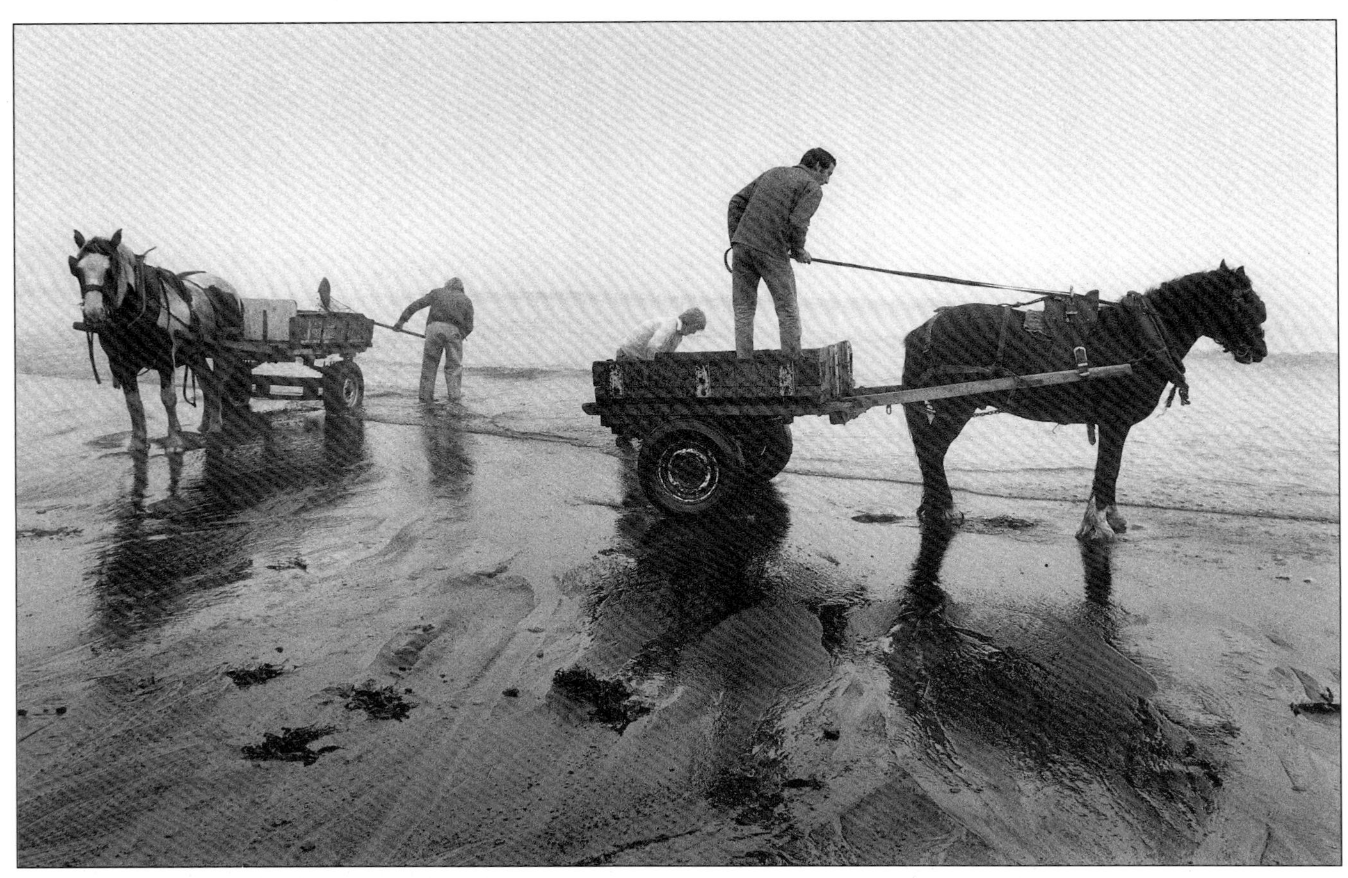

*Sea-coalers, Lynemouth*

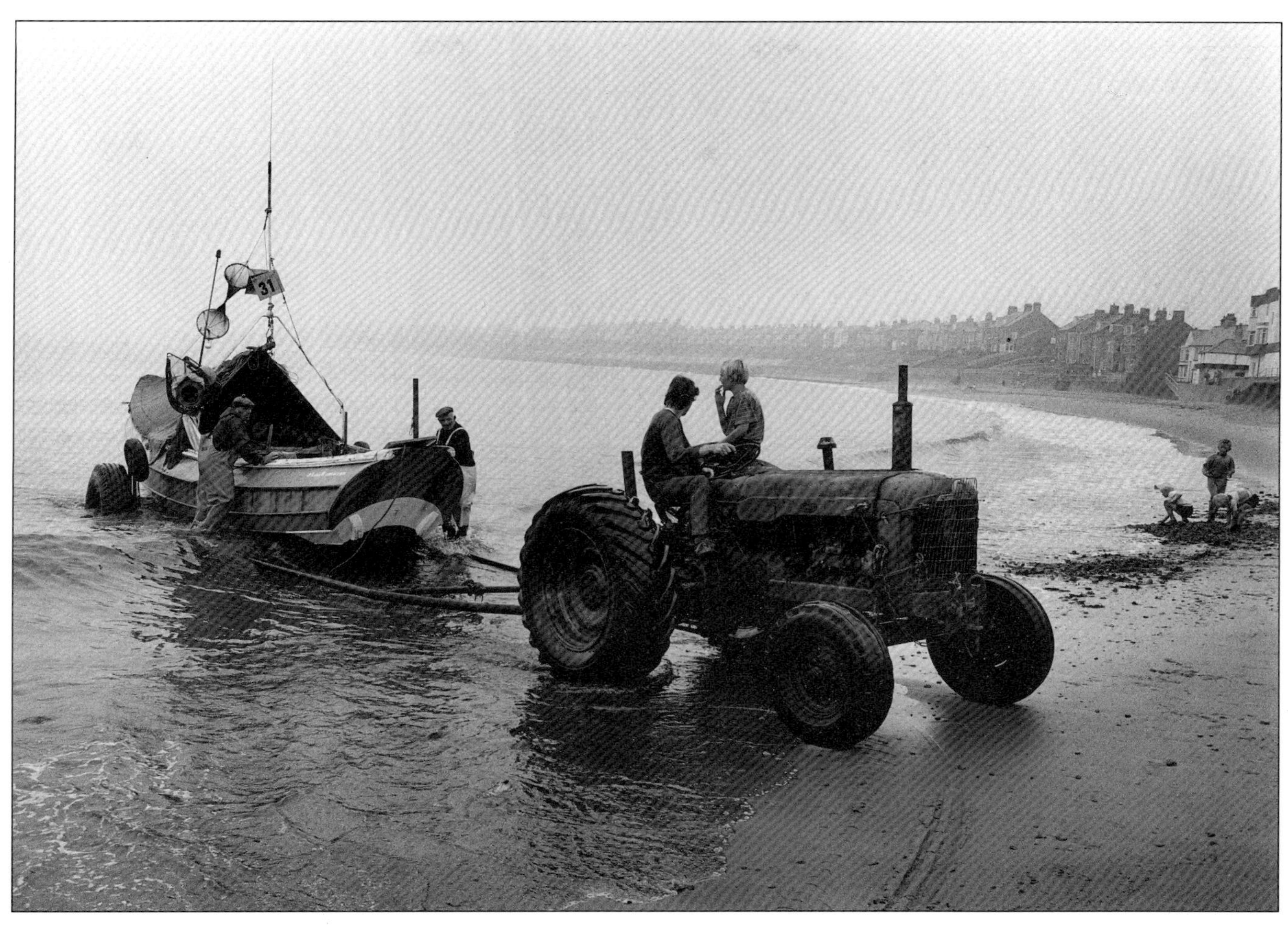


*Fishermen and coble, Newbiggin by the Sea*

*Packing kippers, Craster*

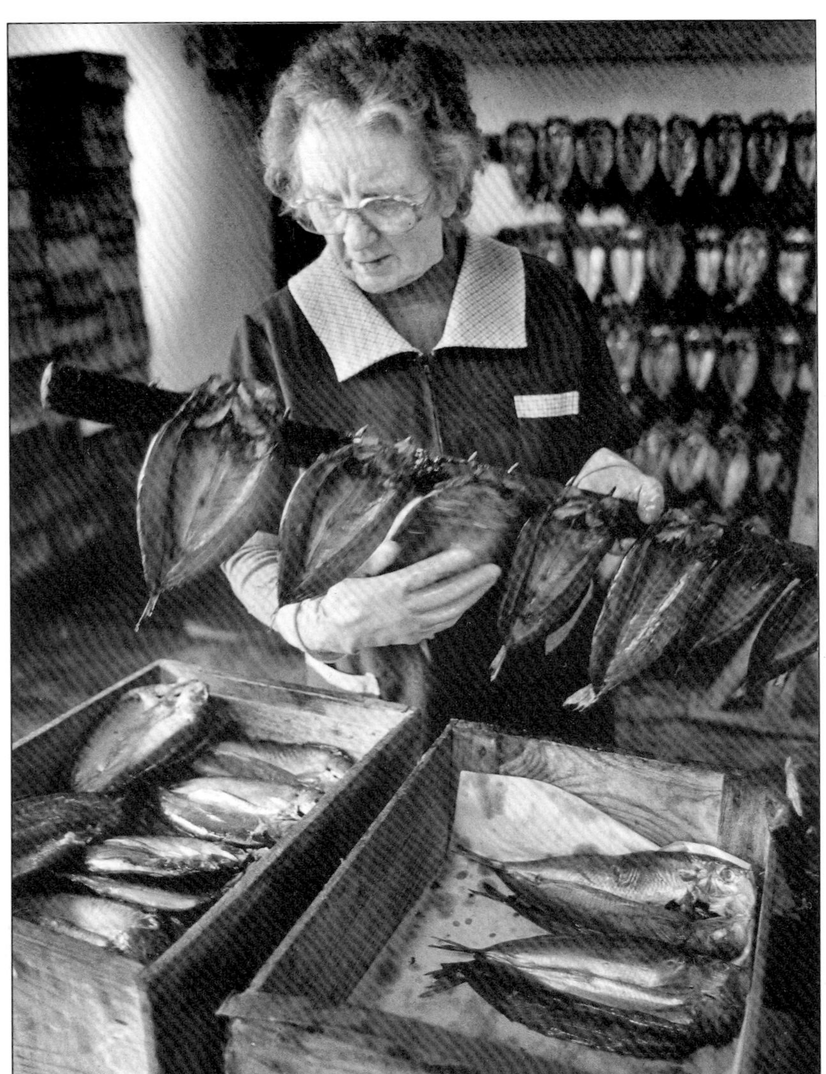

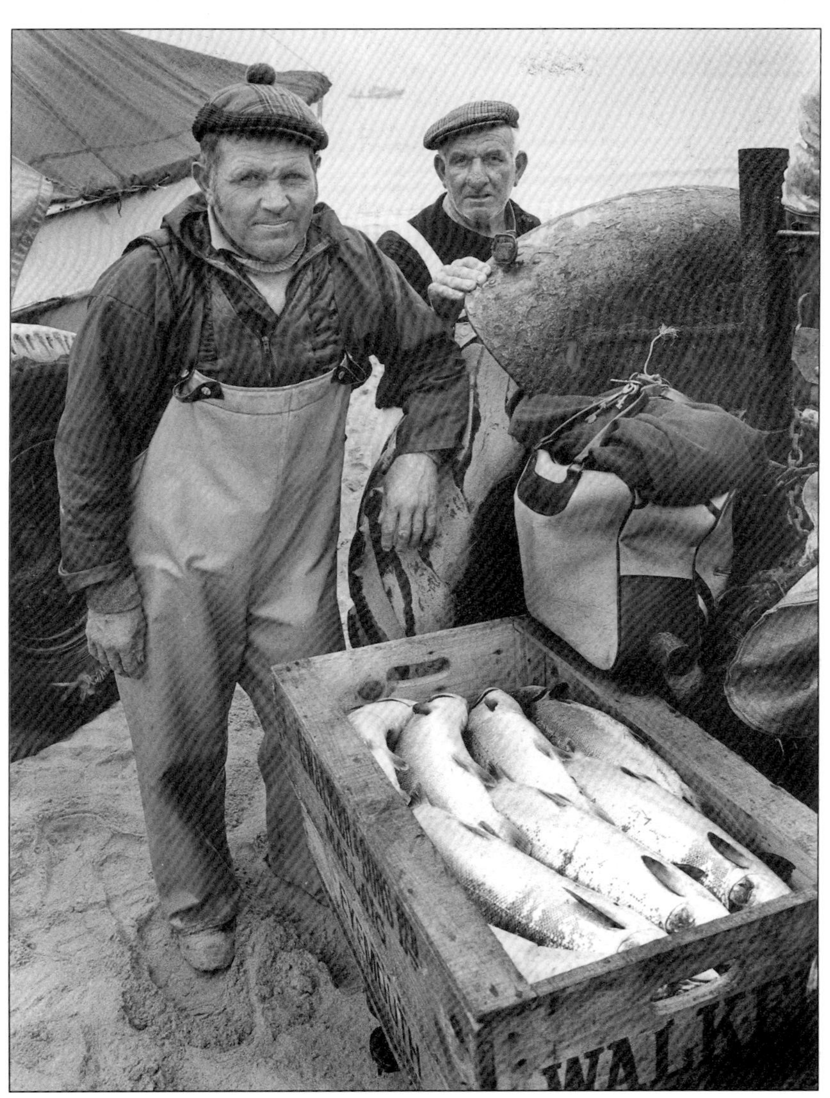


*Fishermen Bobby Dawson & Jackie Lisle Robinson, Newbiggin by the Sea*

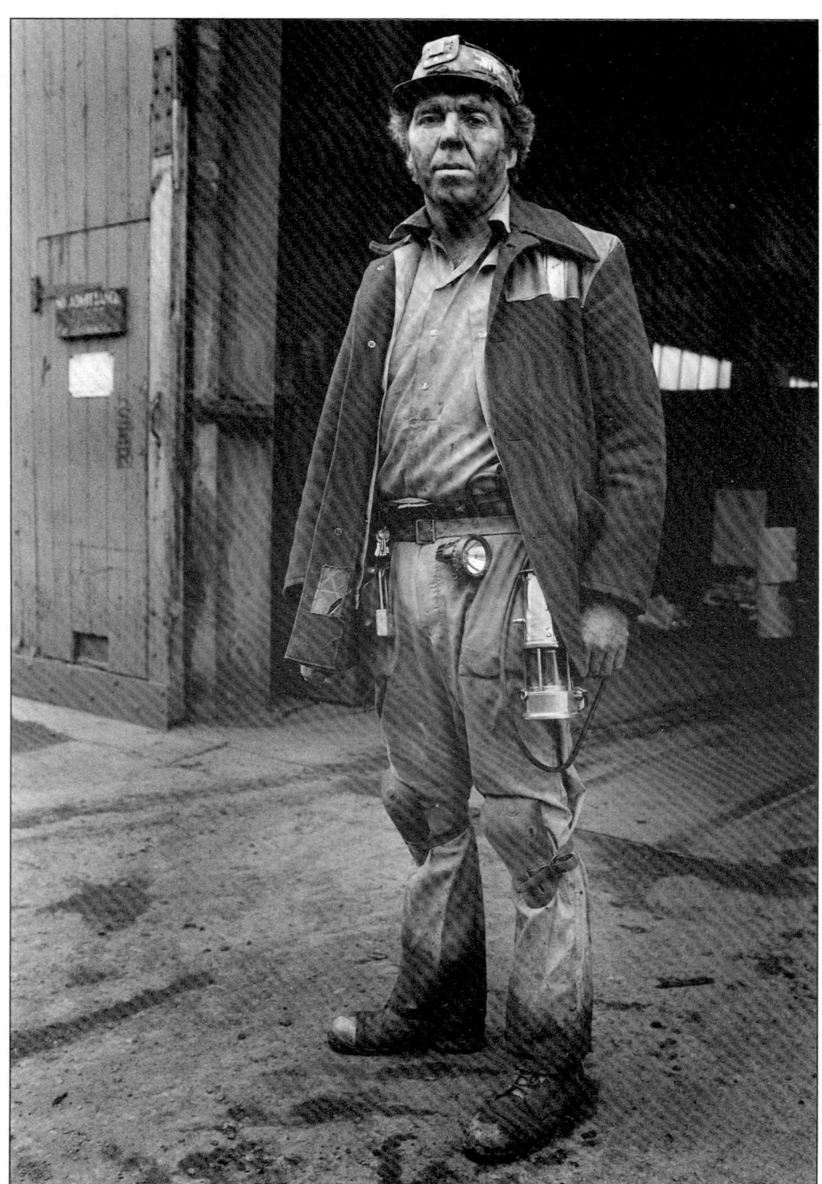

*Pit Deputy Derek Longstaff, Ashington Colliery*

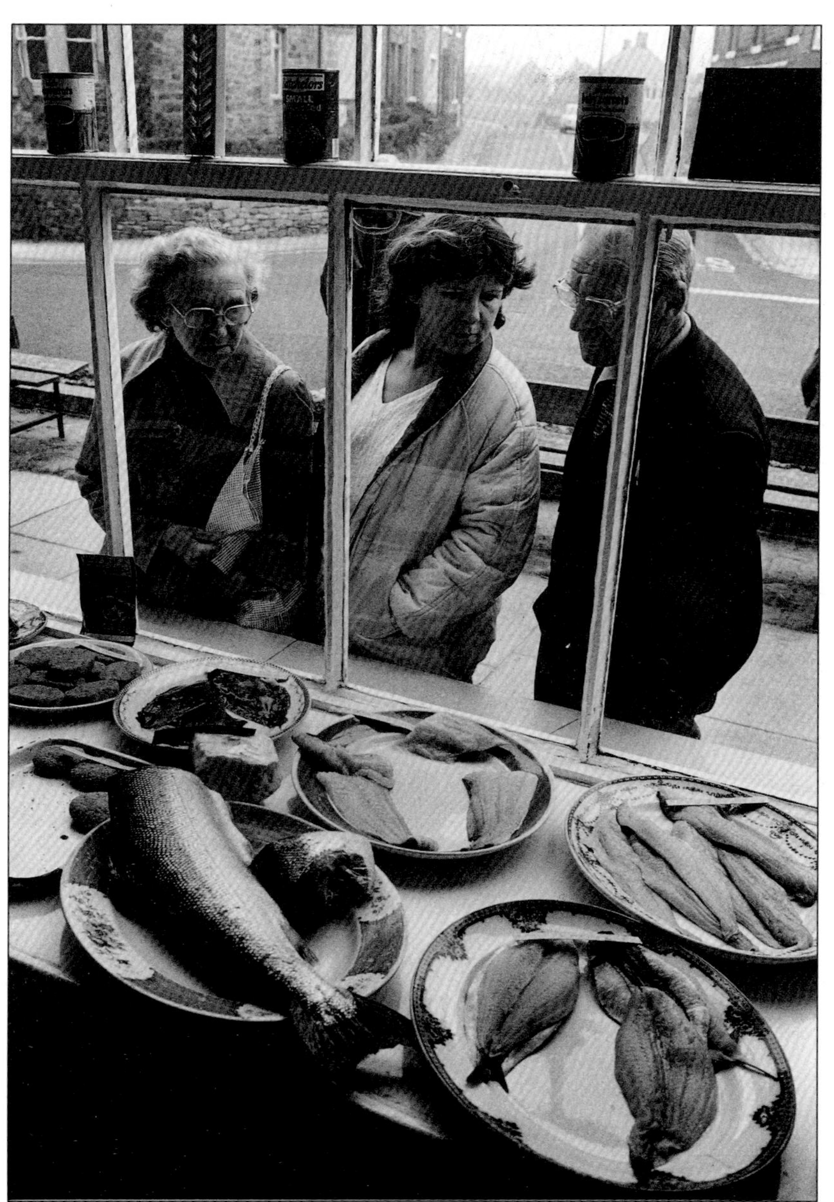

*The fish shop, Newbiggin by the Sea*

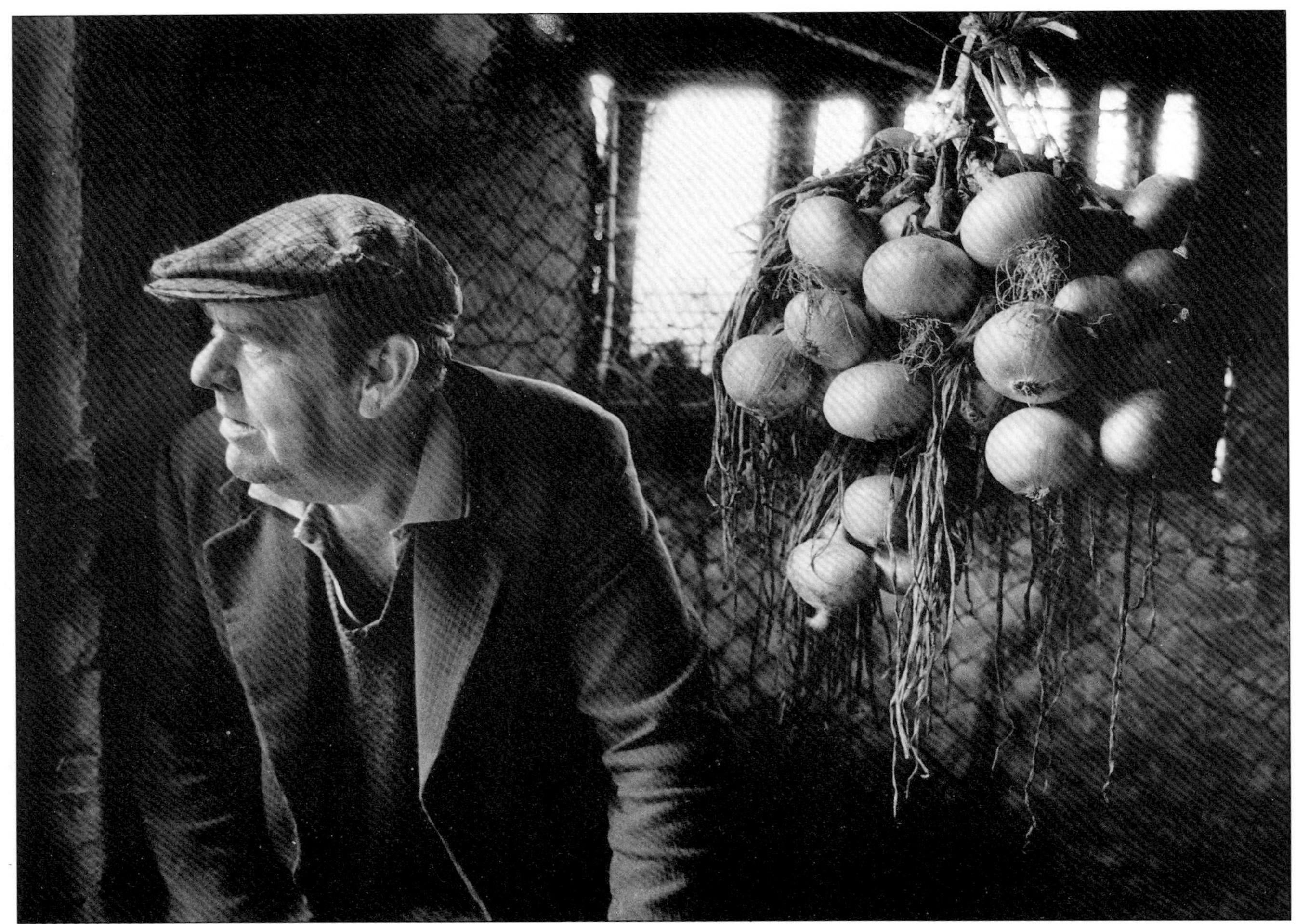

*Matty Callan, Newbiggin by the Sea*

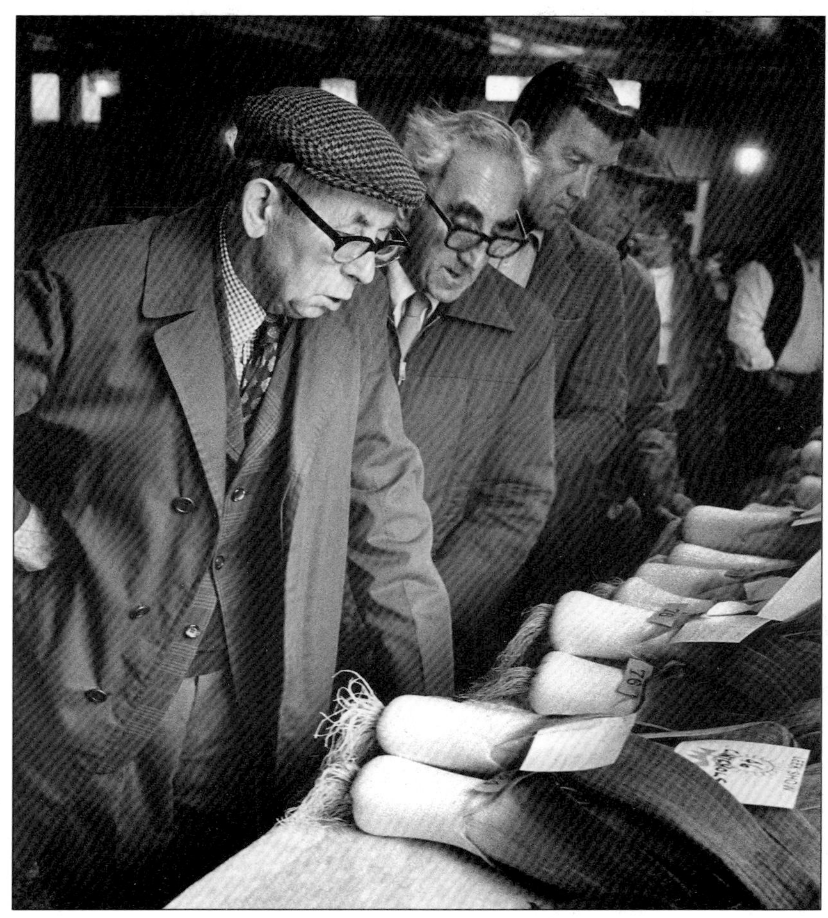

*Leek Show, Central Club, Newbiggin by the Sea*

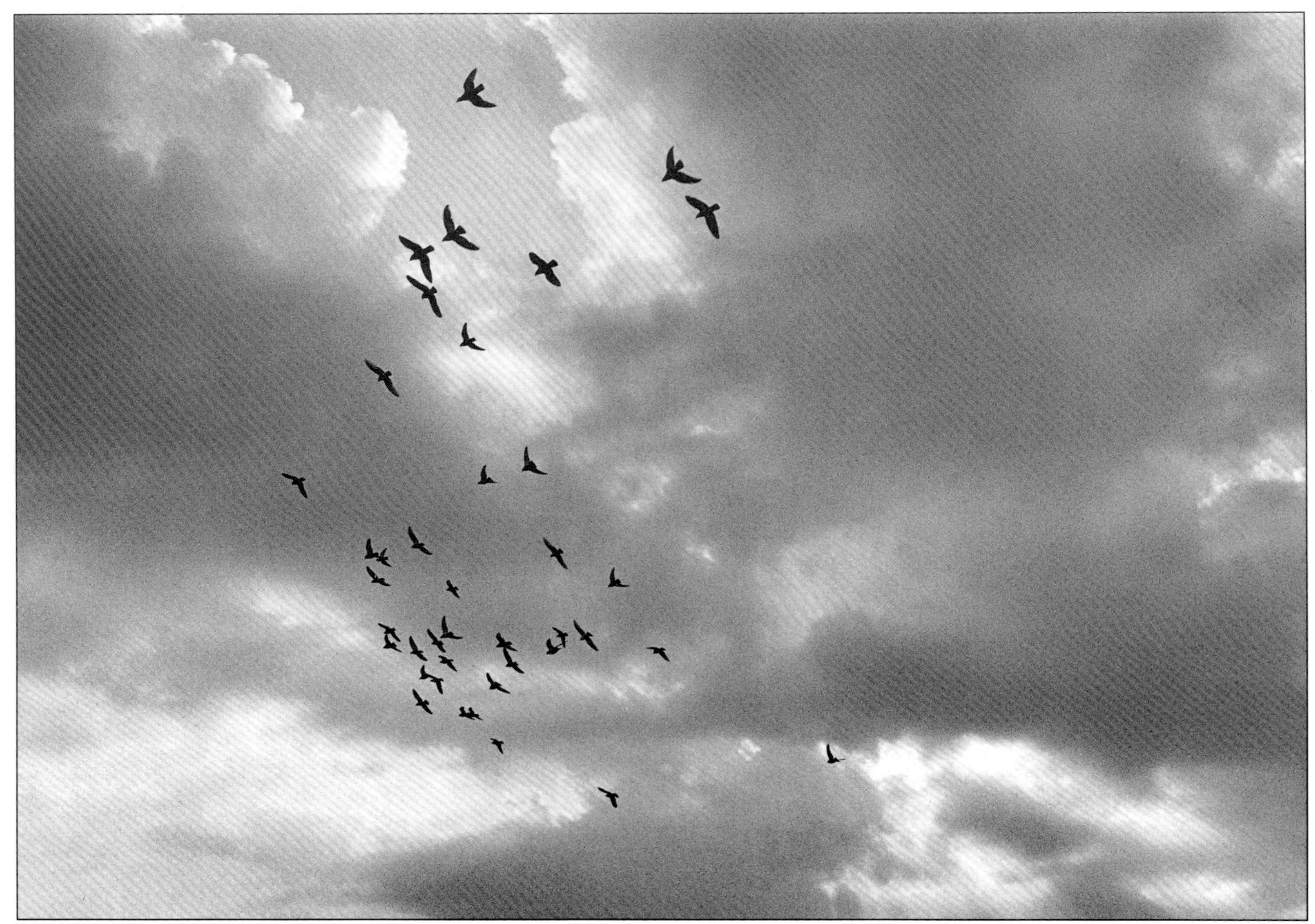

*Homing pigeons*

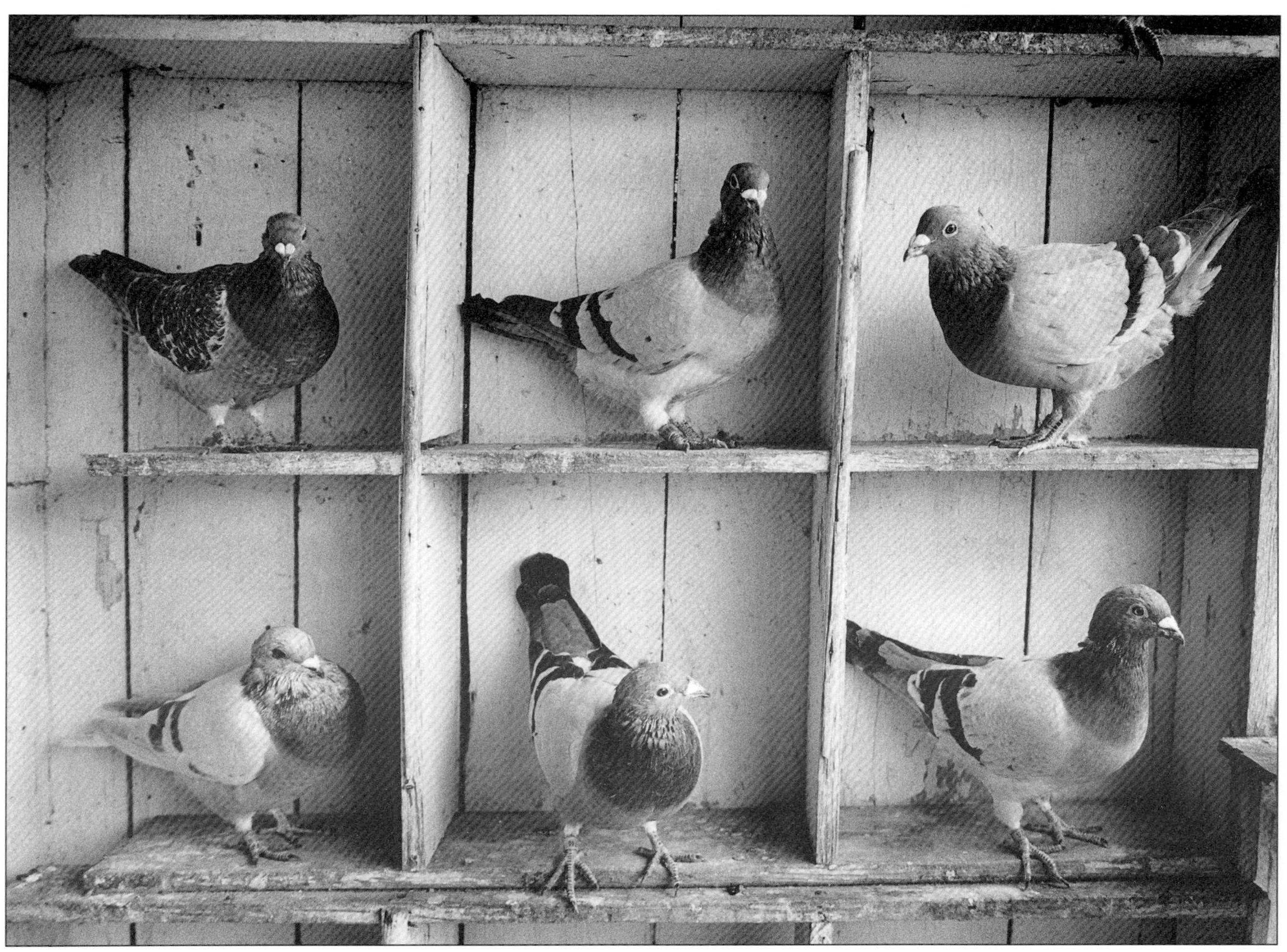

*Homing pigeons in their allotment cree*

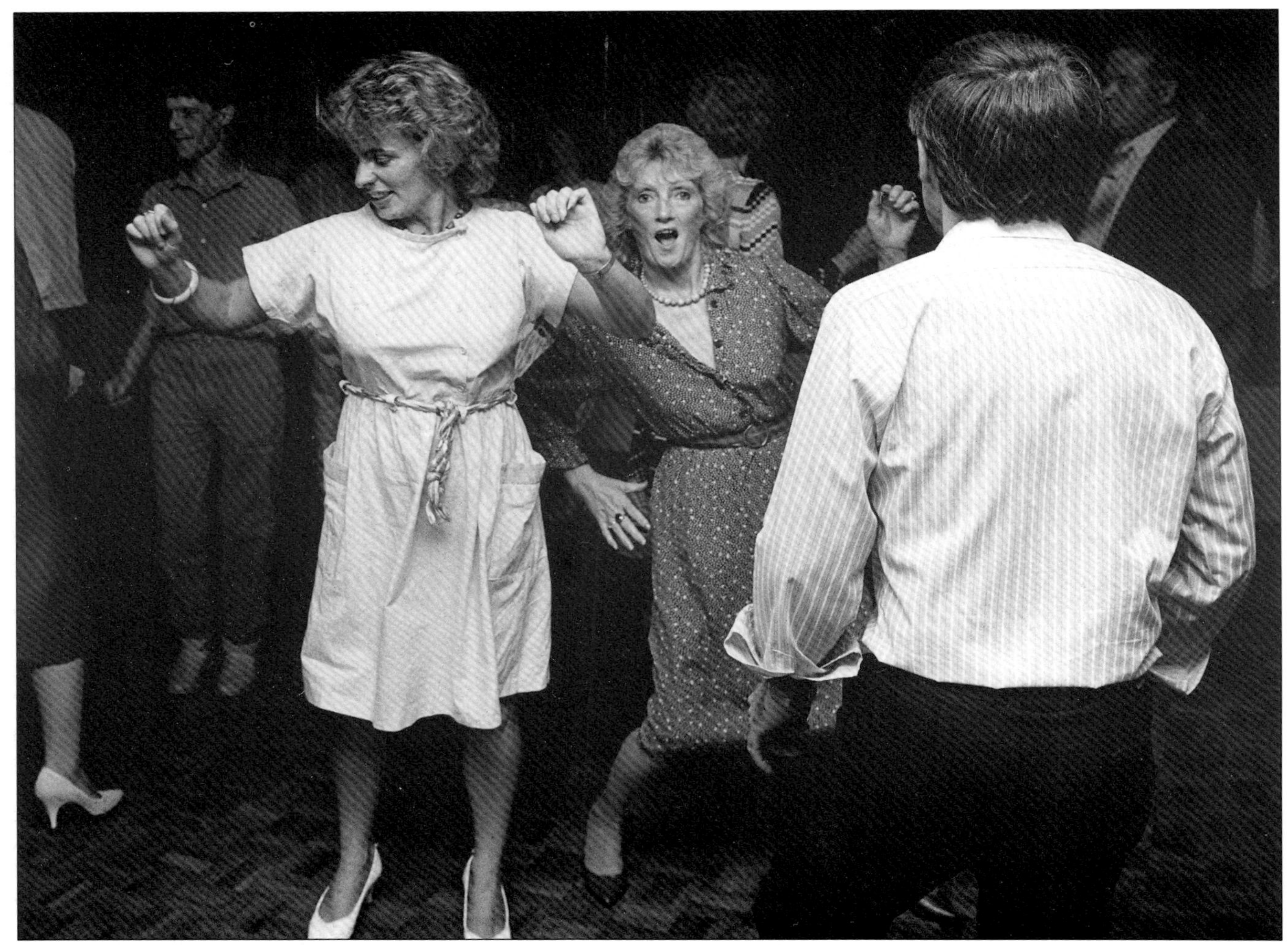

*Saturday night dance, Bank Top Club, Newbiggin by the Sea*

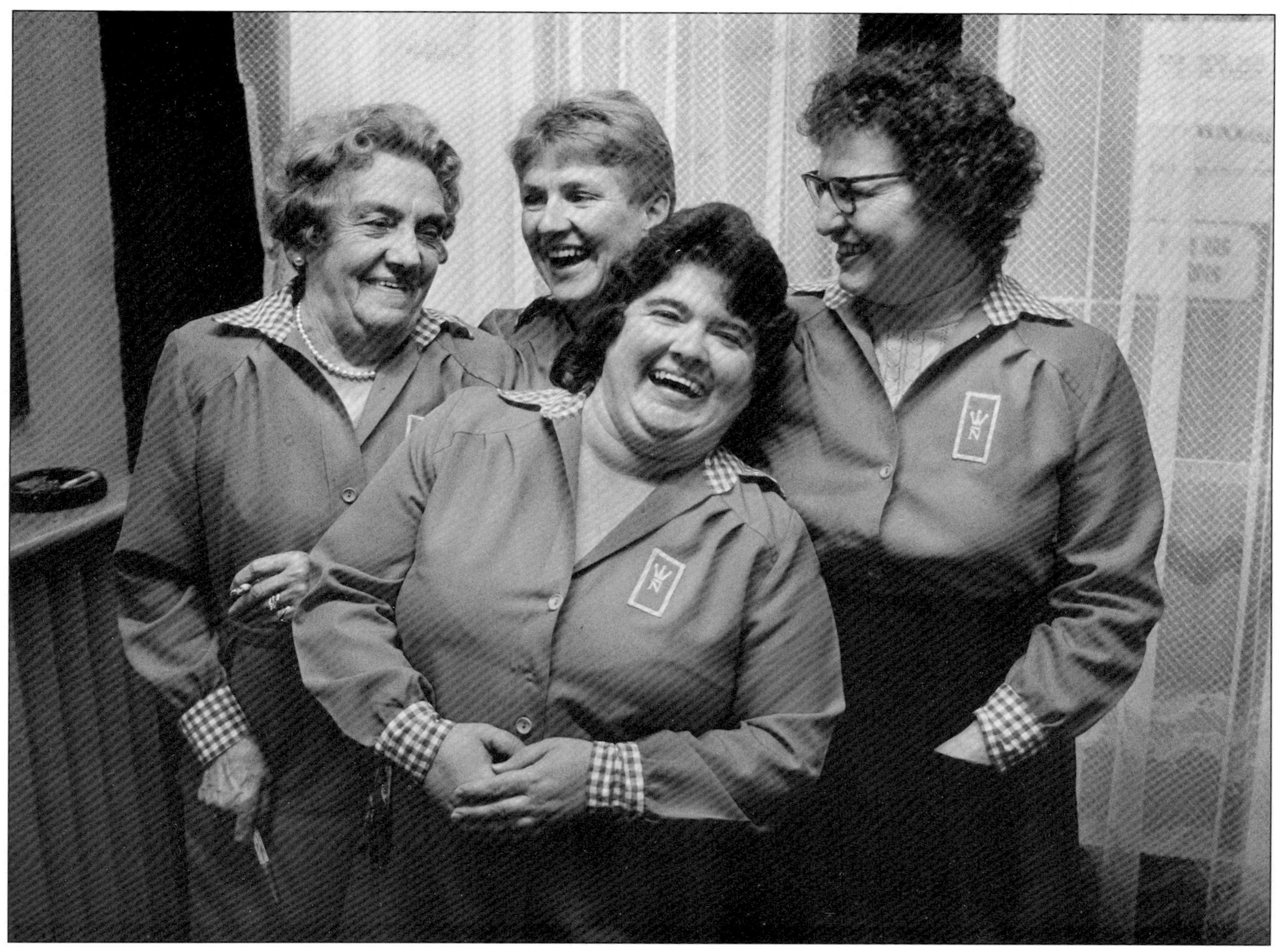

*Bingo hall attendants Carol O'Connell (front), Lizzie Davidson, Isobel Dent & Bet McMurdo, Newbiggin by the Sea*

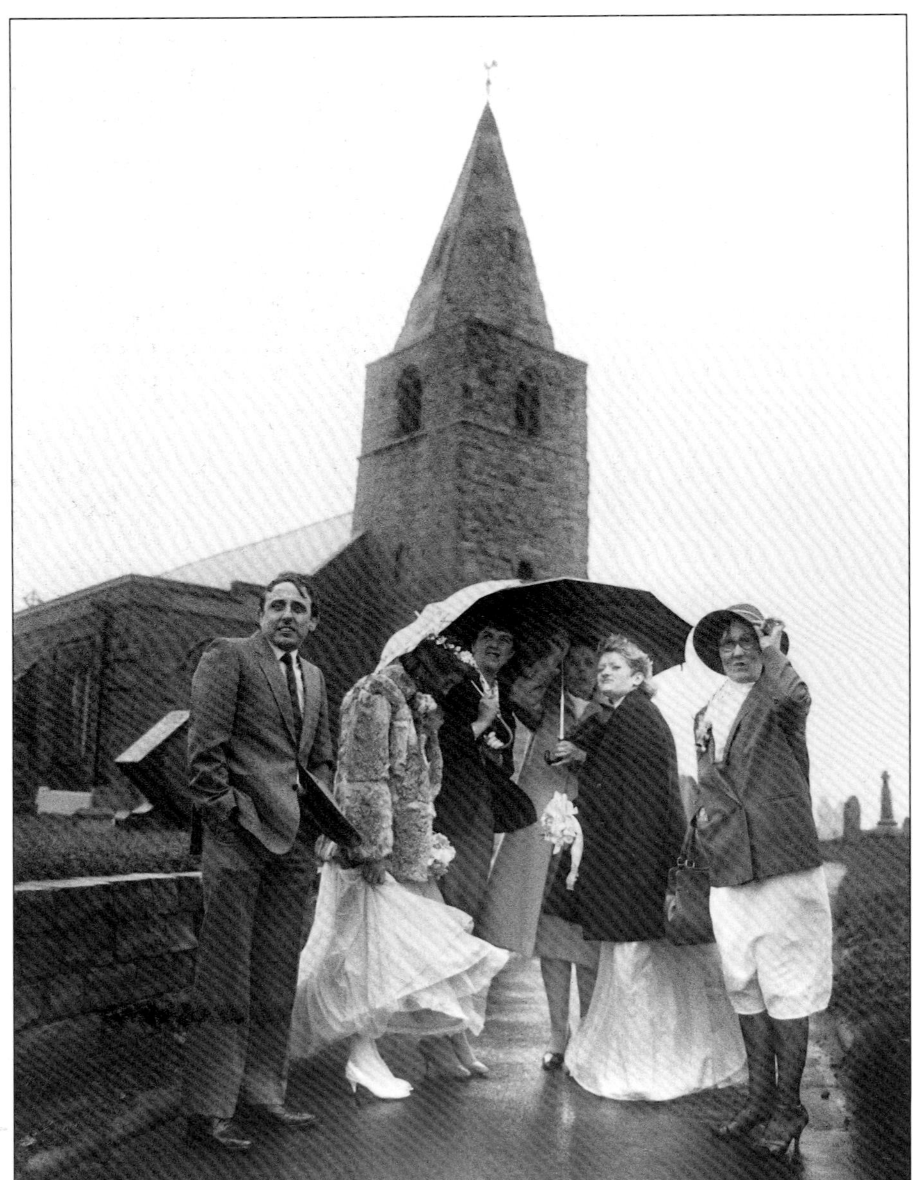

*Wedding party, St Bartholomew's Church, Newbiggin by the Sea*

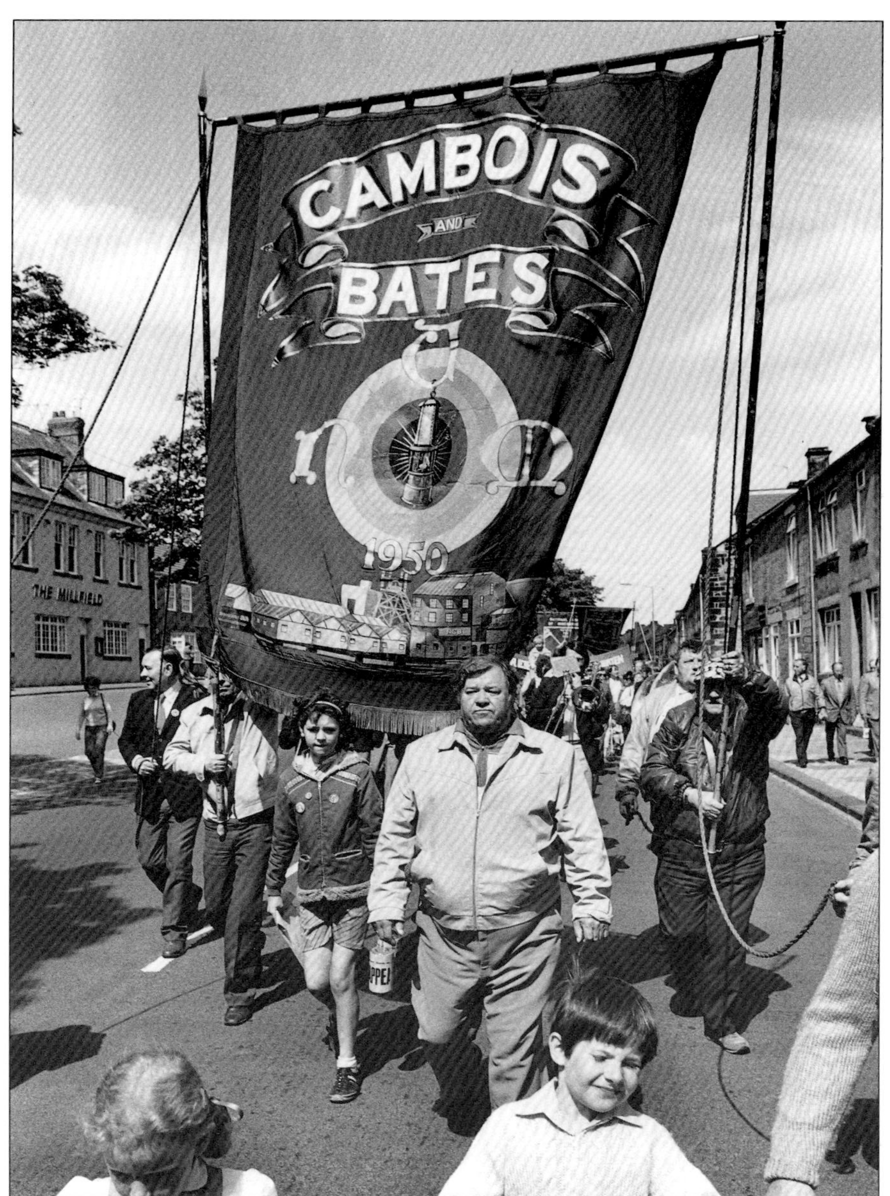


*Miners' march, Bedlington, in protest at the proposed closure of the Bates Pit*

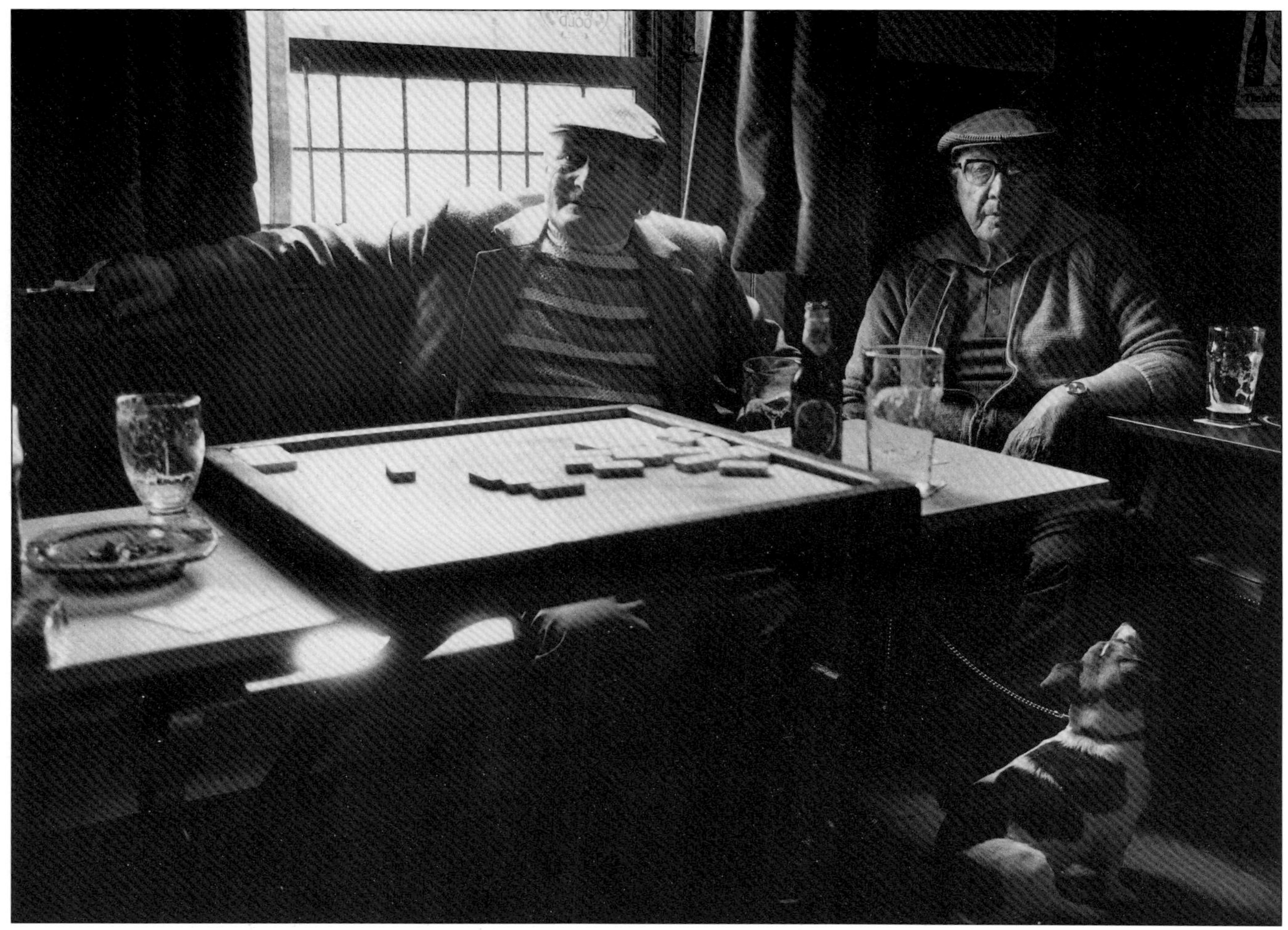

*The Railway Inn, Newbiggin by the Sea*

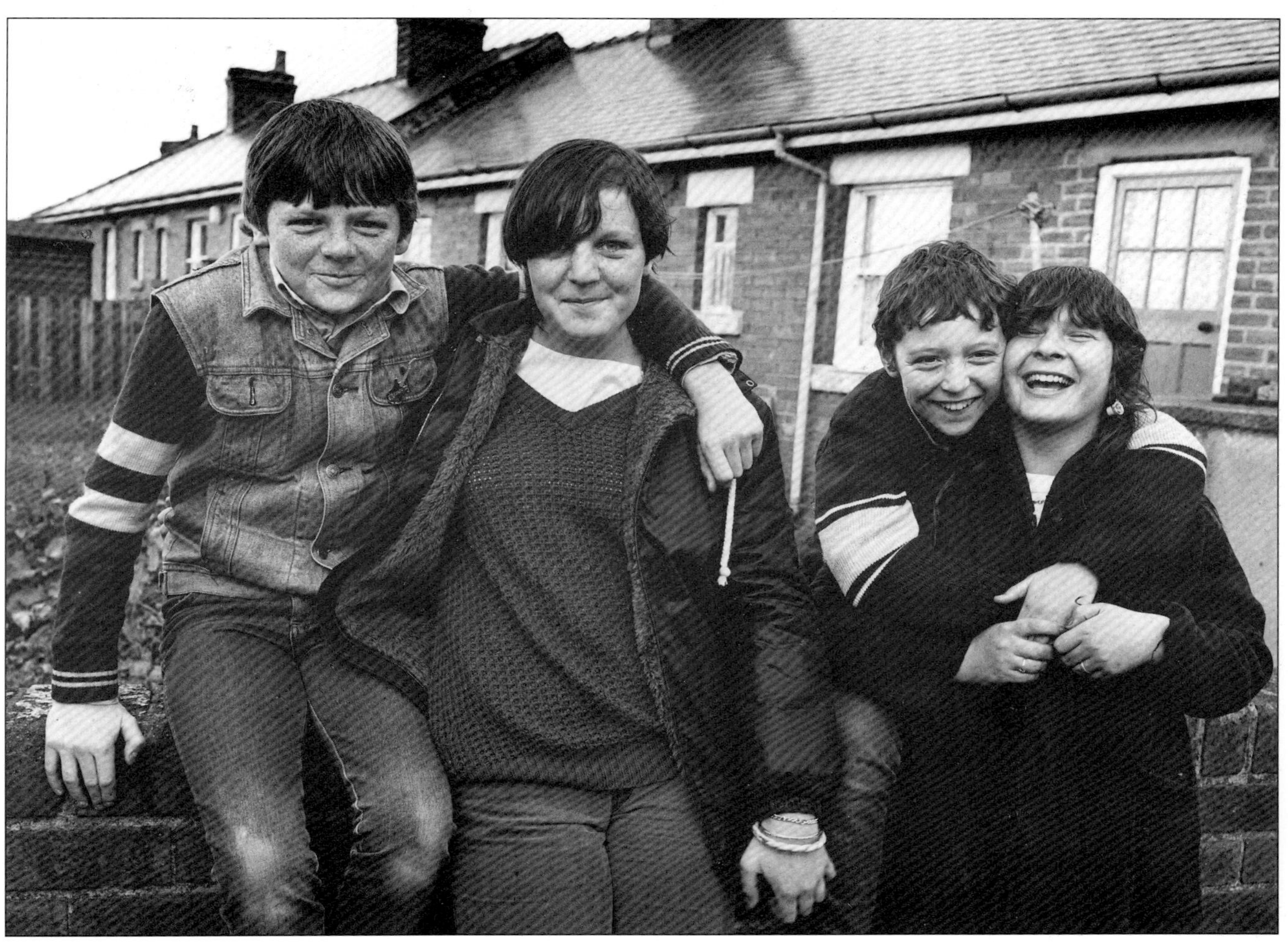

*Teenagers, Newbiggin by the Sea*

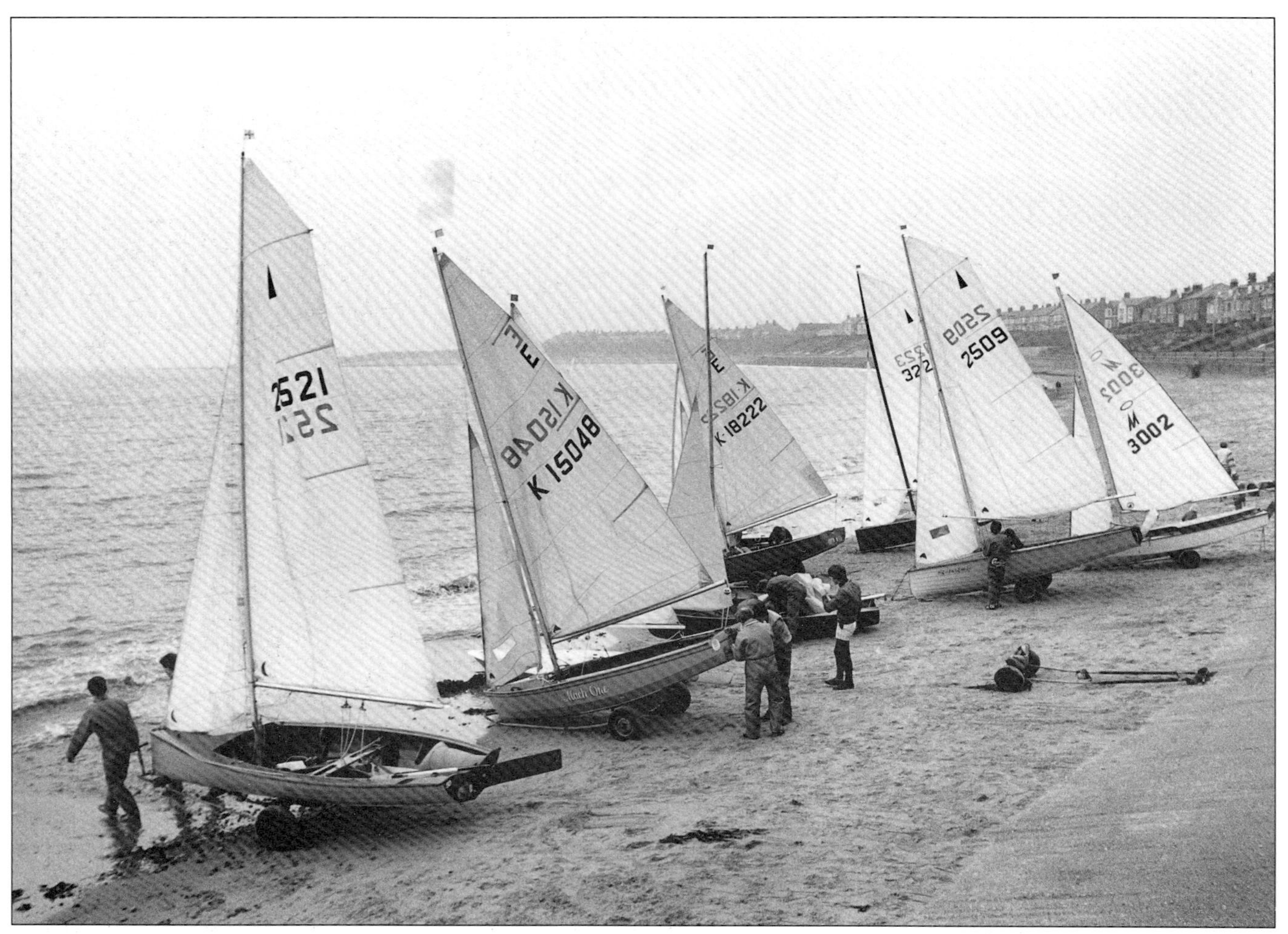


*The sailing club, Newbiggin by the Sea*

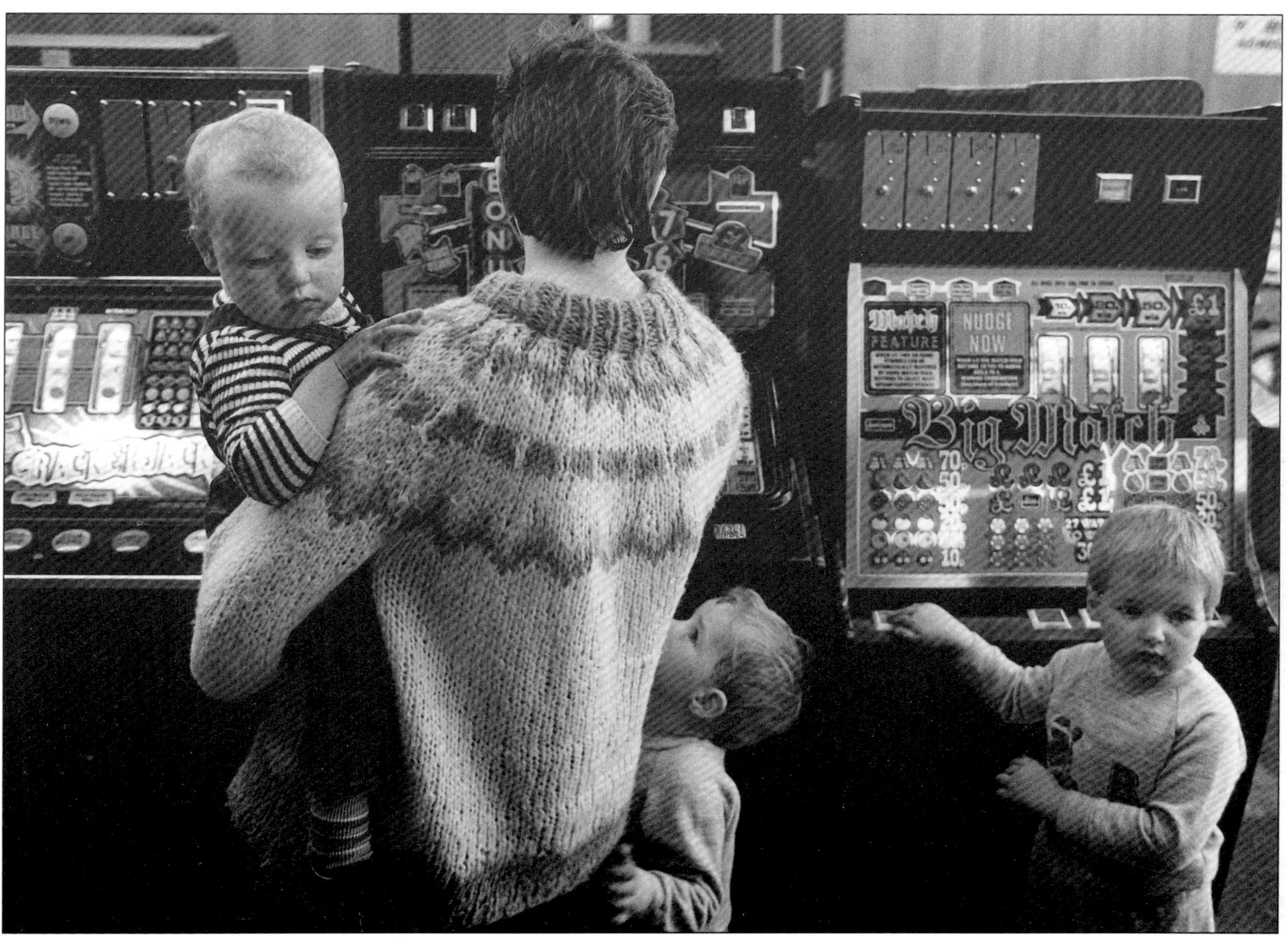


*Amusement arcade, Newbiggin by the Sea*

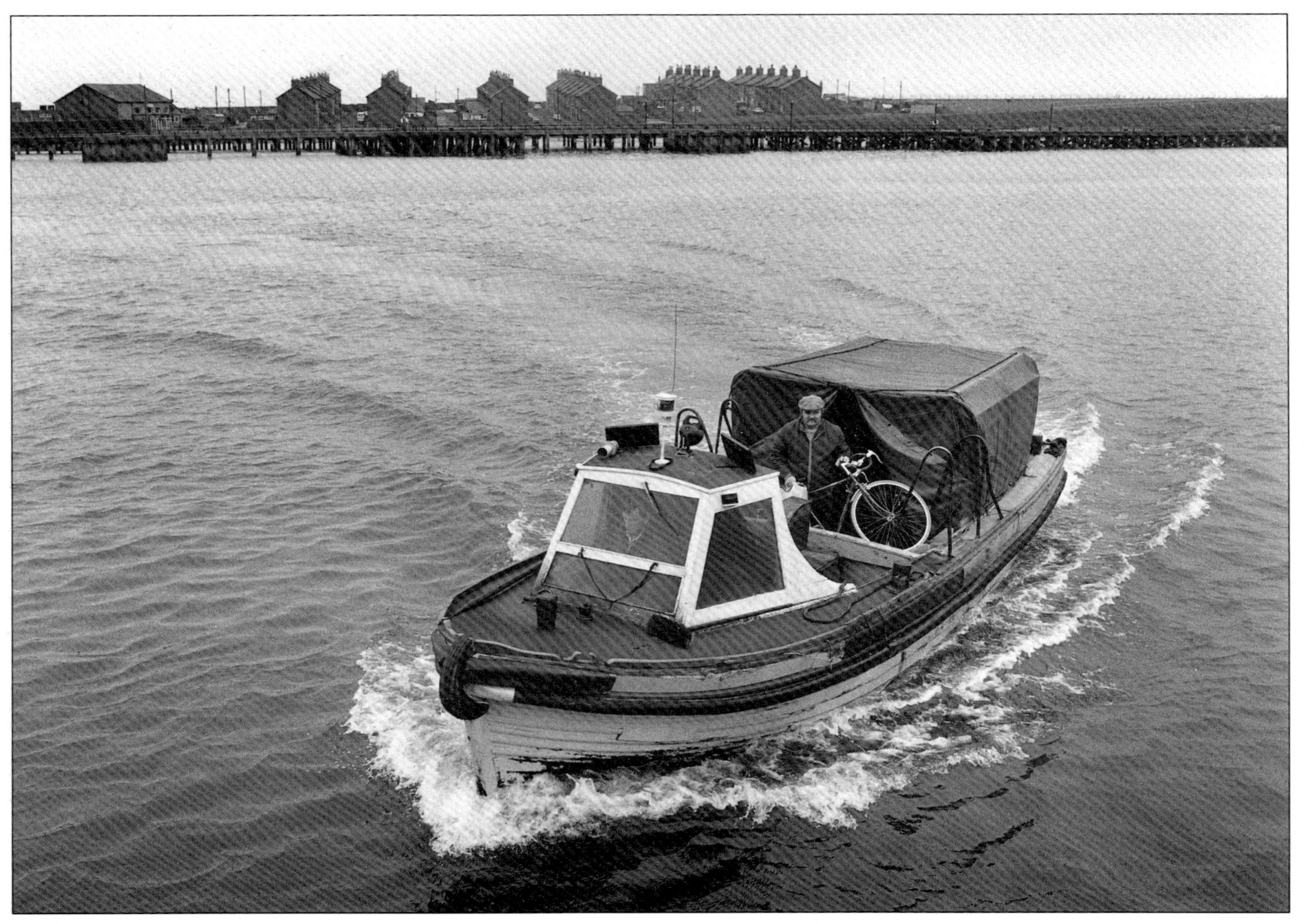

*The ferry between Blyth and North Blyth*

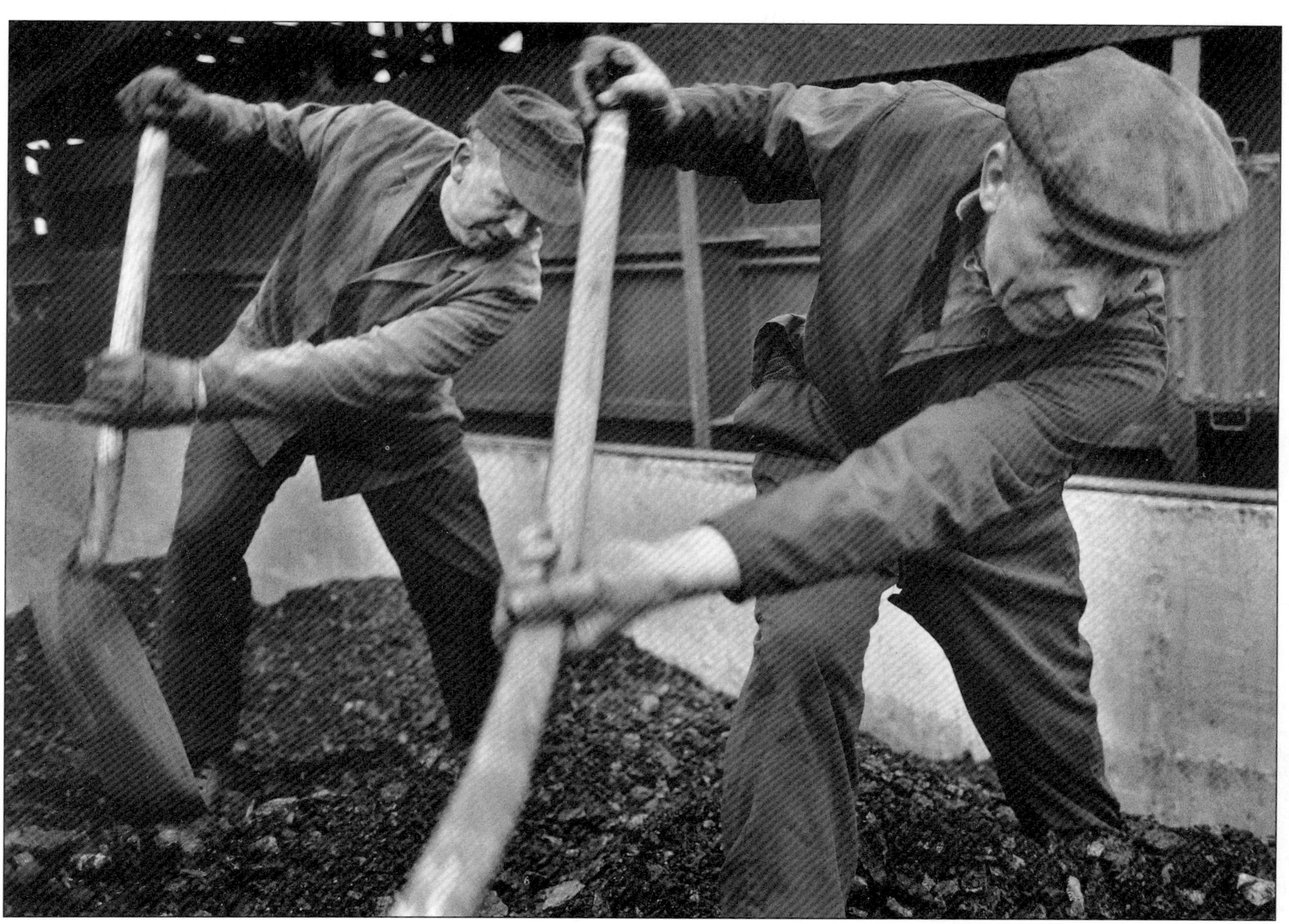

*Coal trimmers, Blyth Harbour*

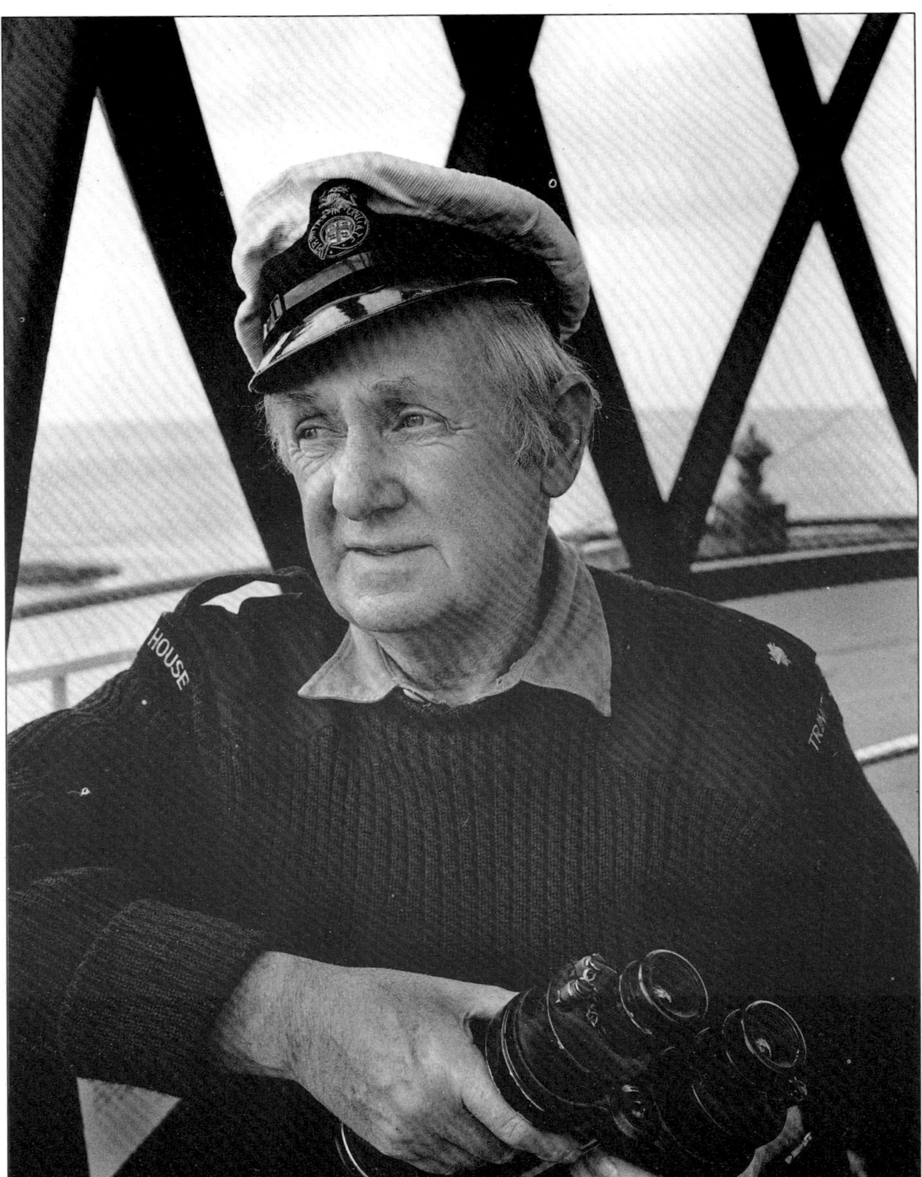


*John Malcolm Macpherson, principal keeper of the Longstone Lighthouse, Farne Islands*

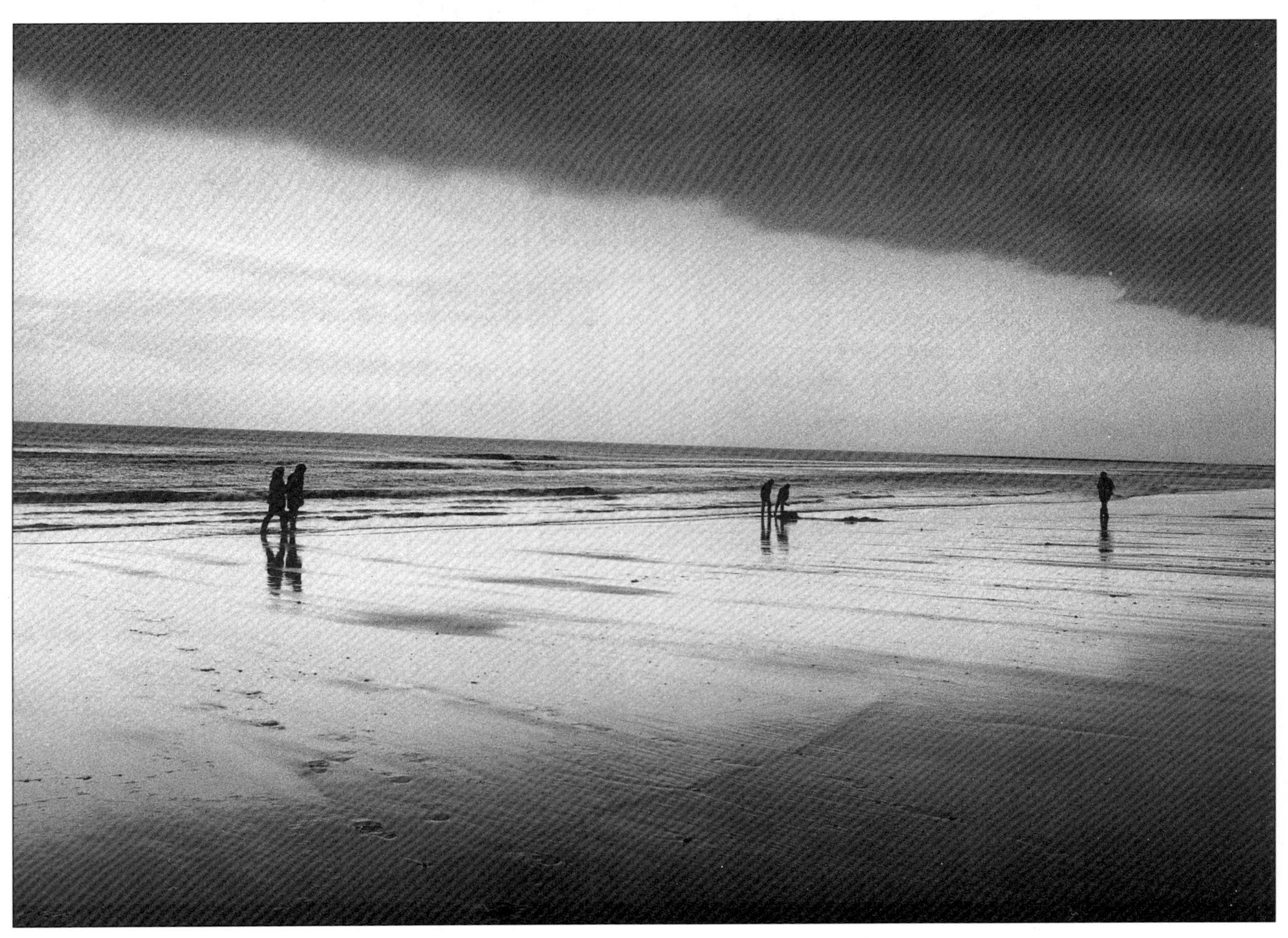

*Druridge Bay*

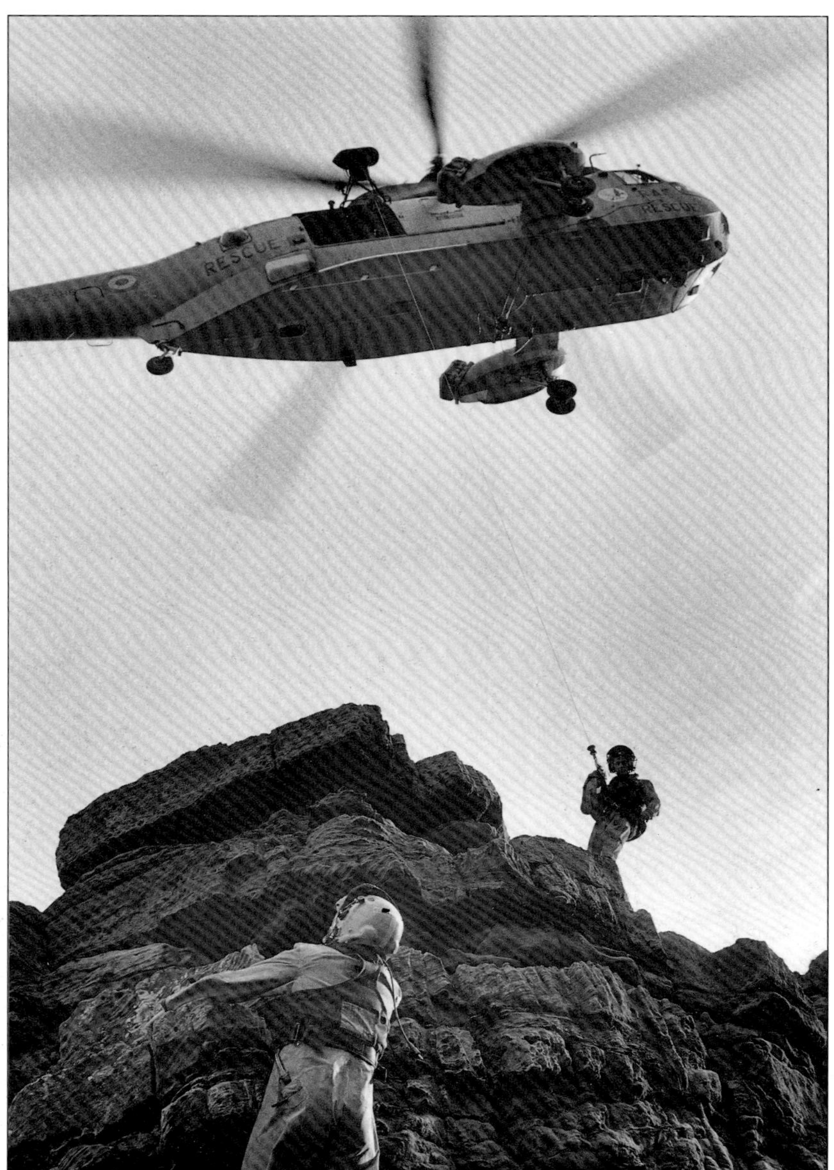


*RAF rescue practice, near Boulmer*

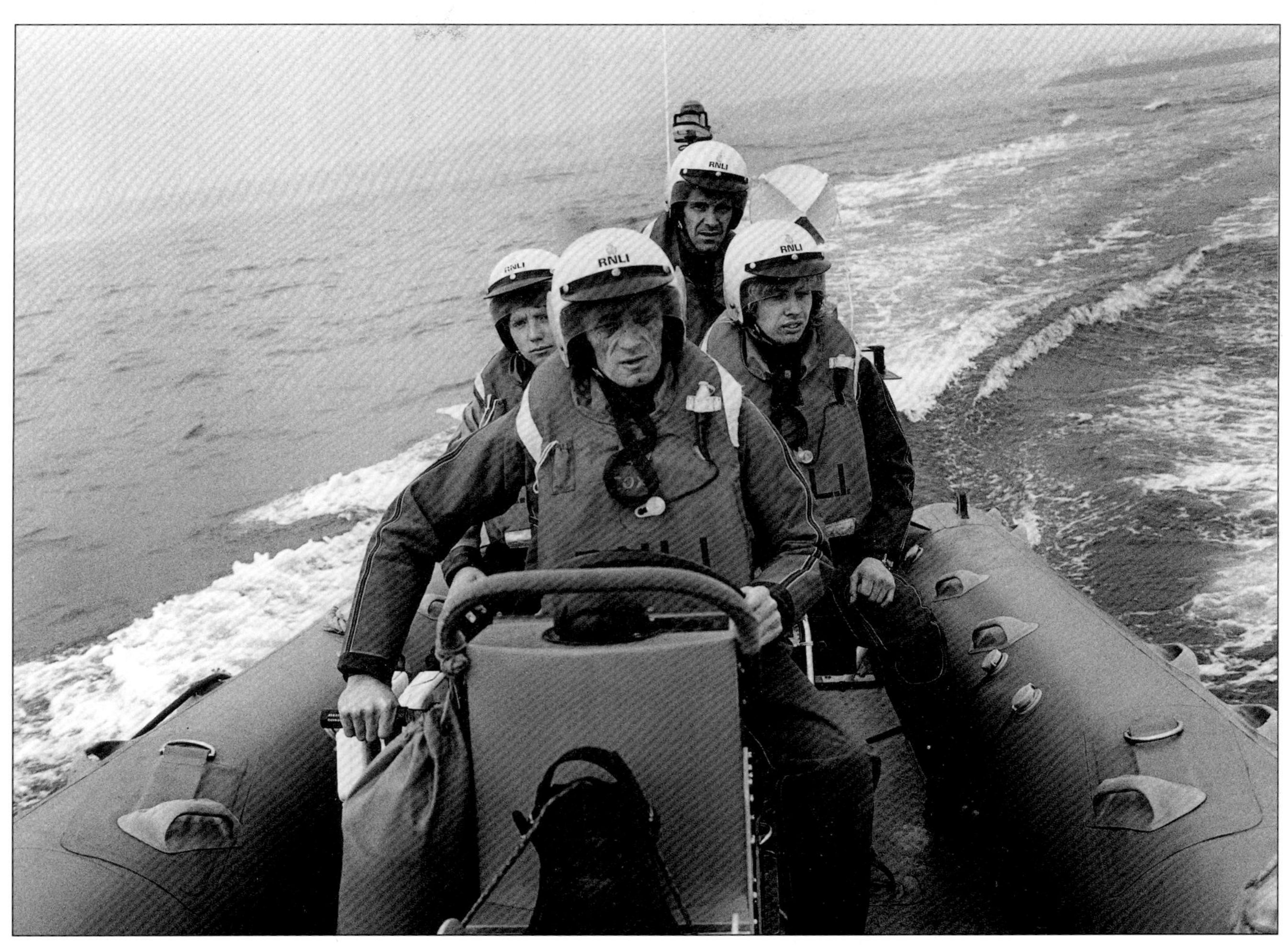


*RNLI inshore rescue practice, Newbiggin by the Sea*

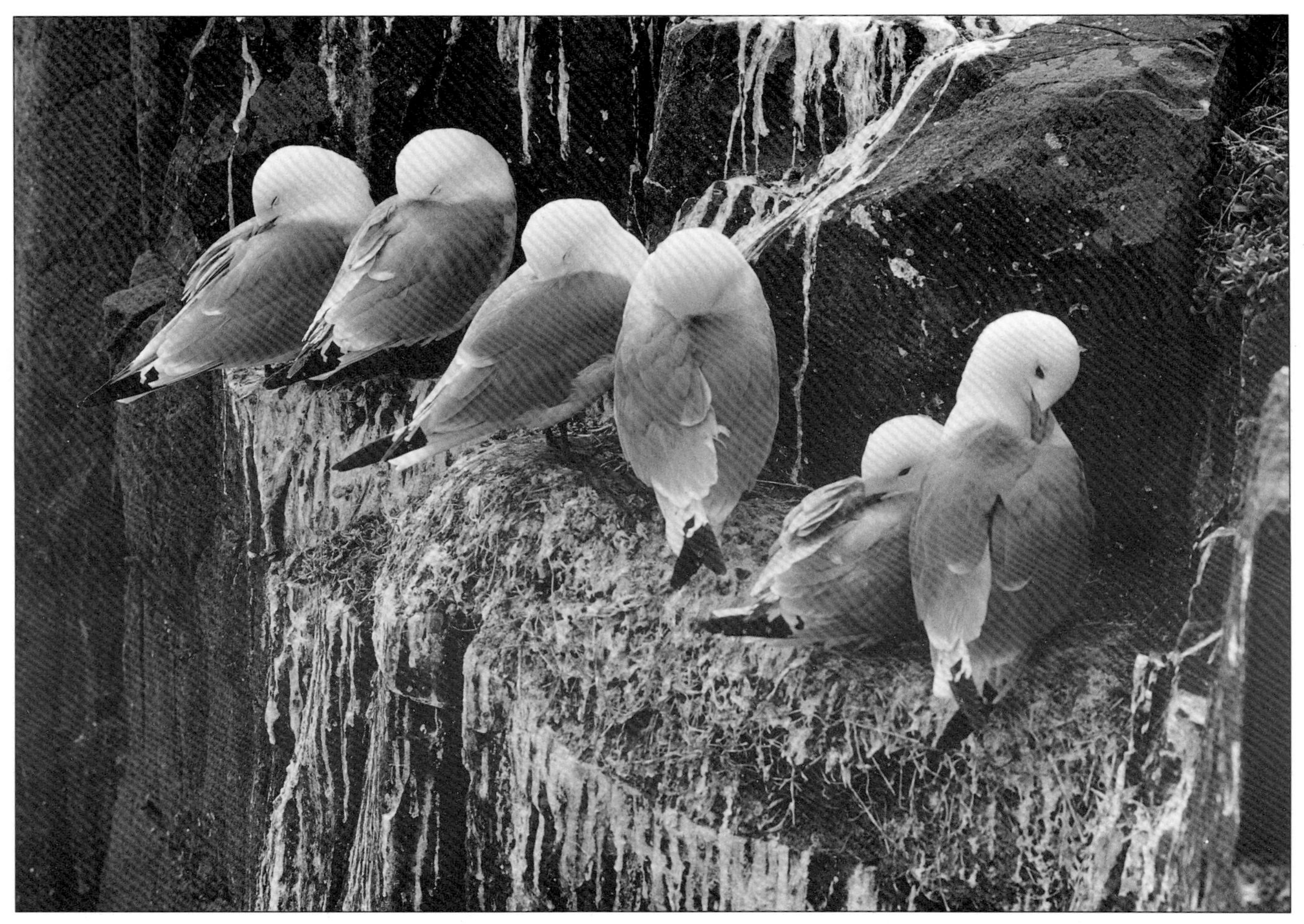

*Kittiwakes, Farne Islands*

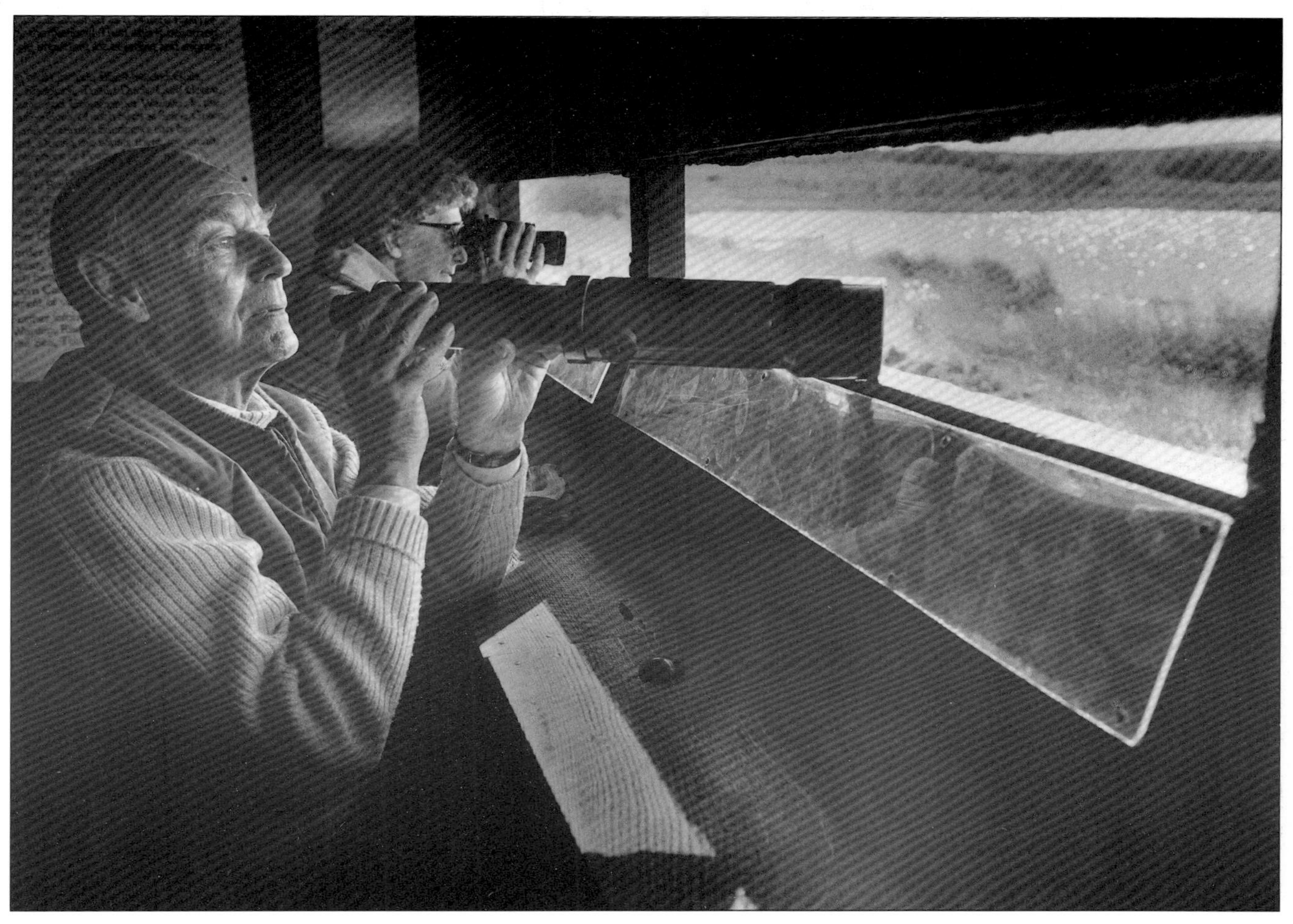

*The National Trust's hide at Newton Pool*

*Alnmouth Friary*

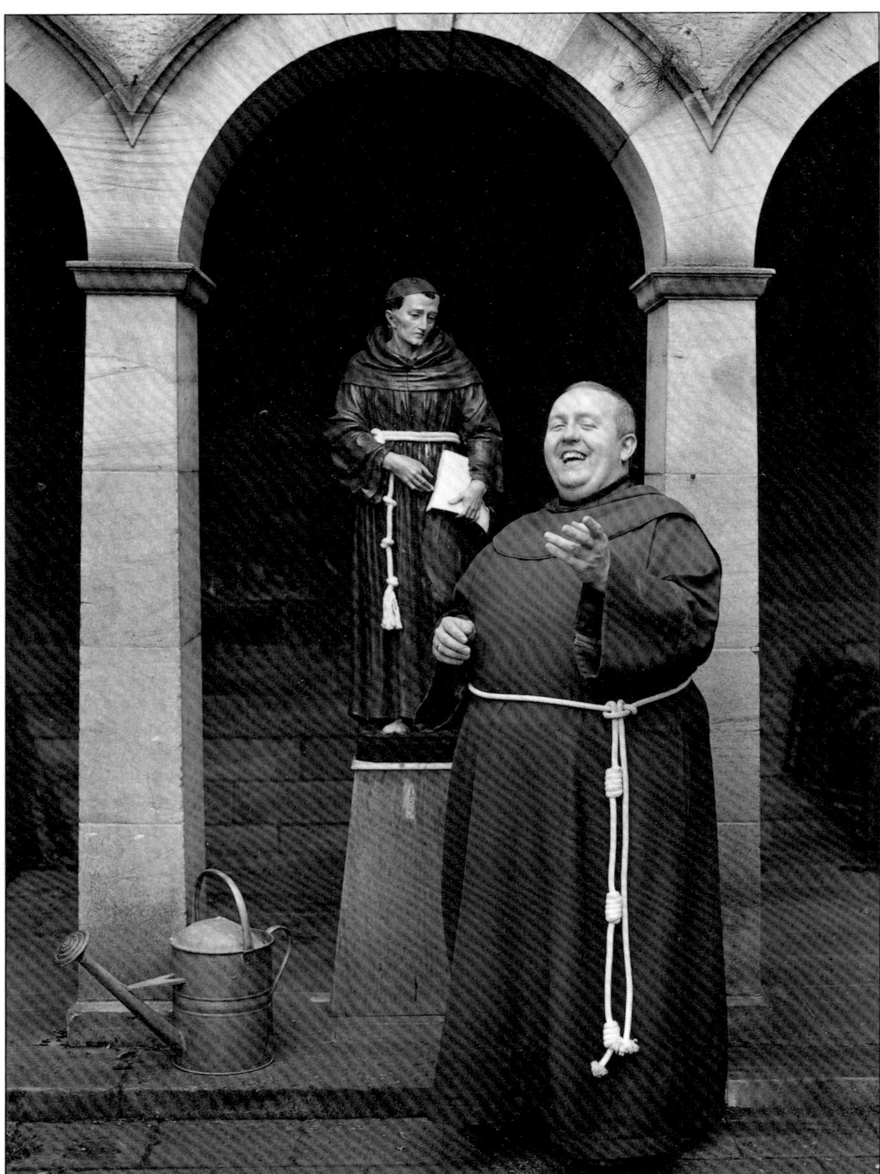

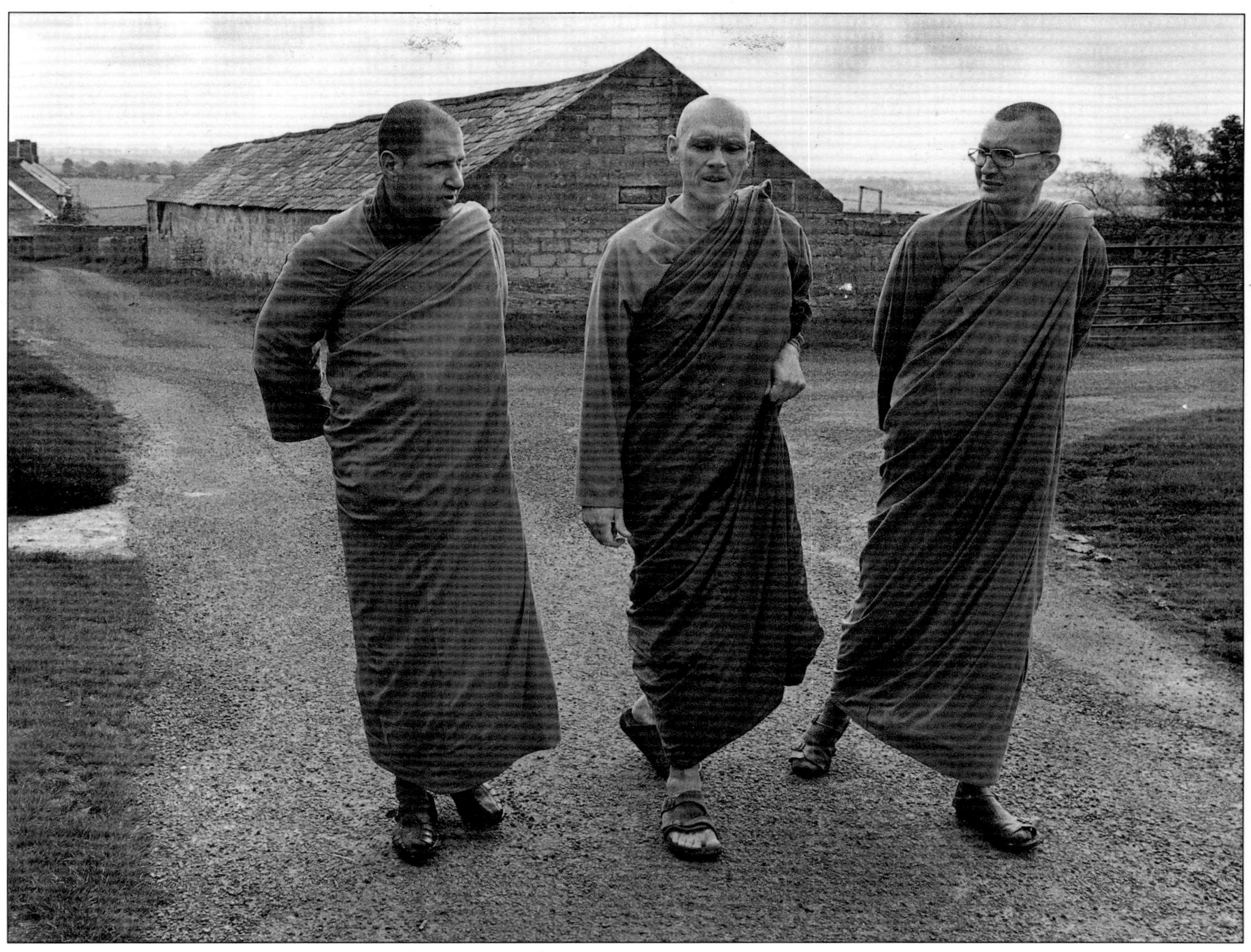

*Harnham Hall Buddhist Monastery, near Belsay*

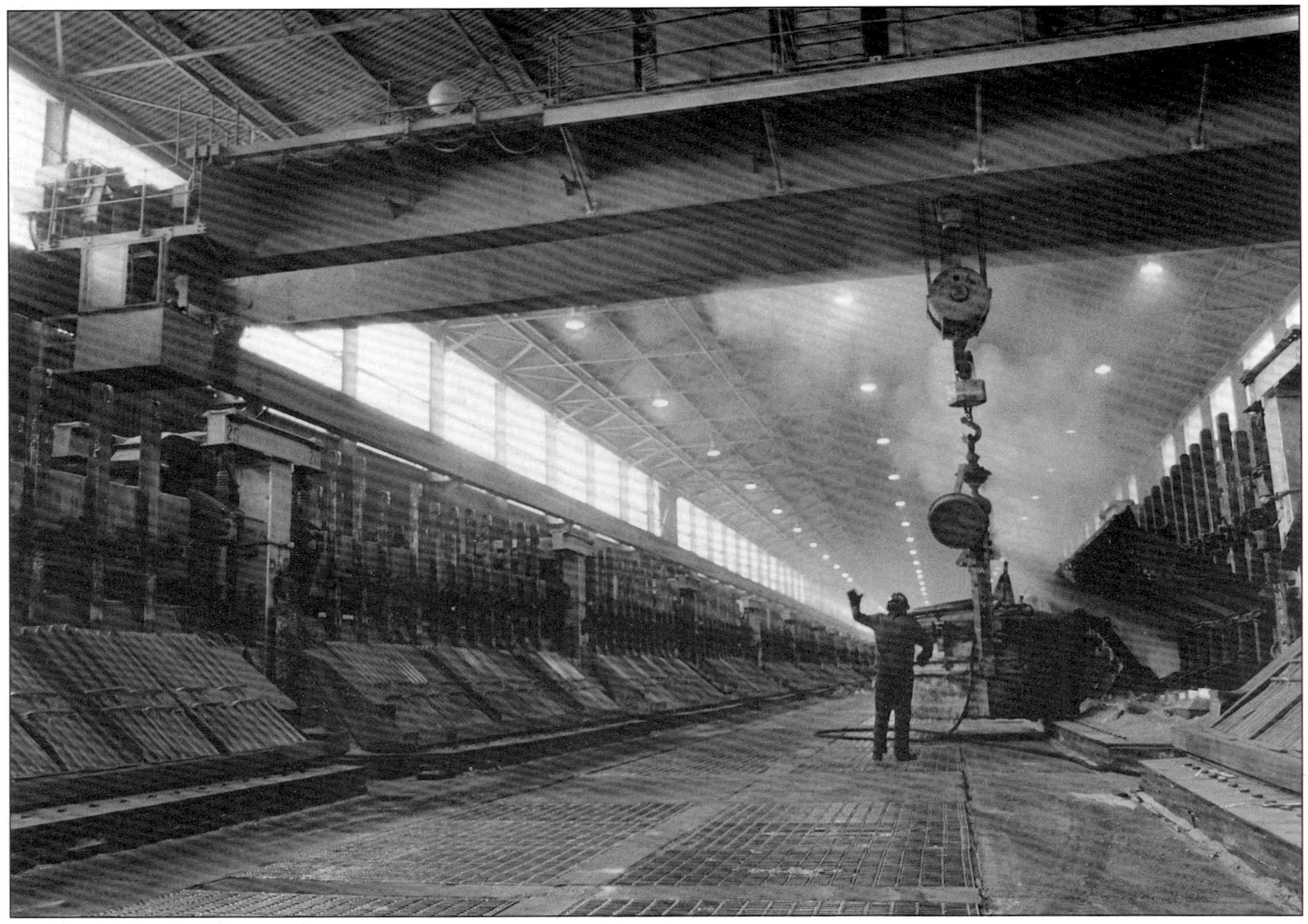

*Alcan's aluminium smelter, Lynemouth*

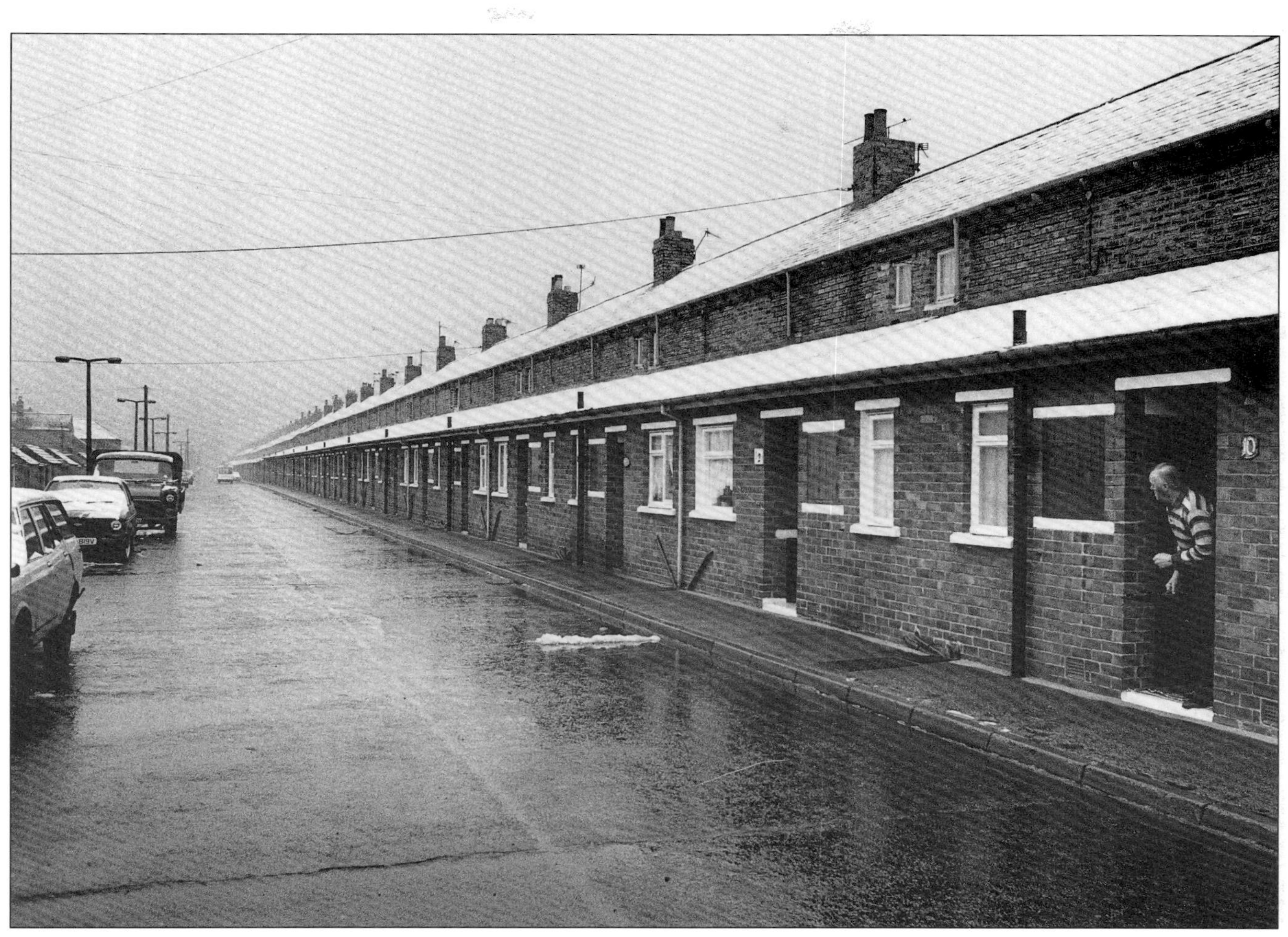

*Chestnut Street, Ashington*

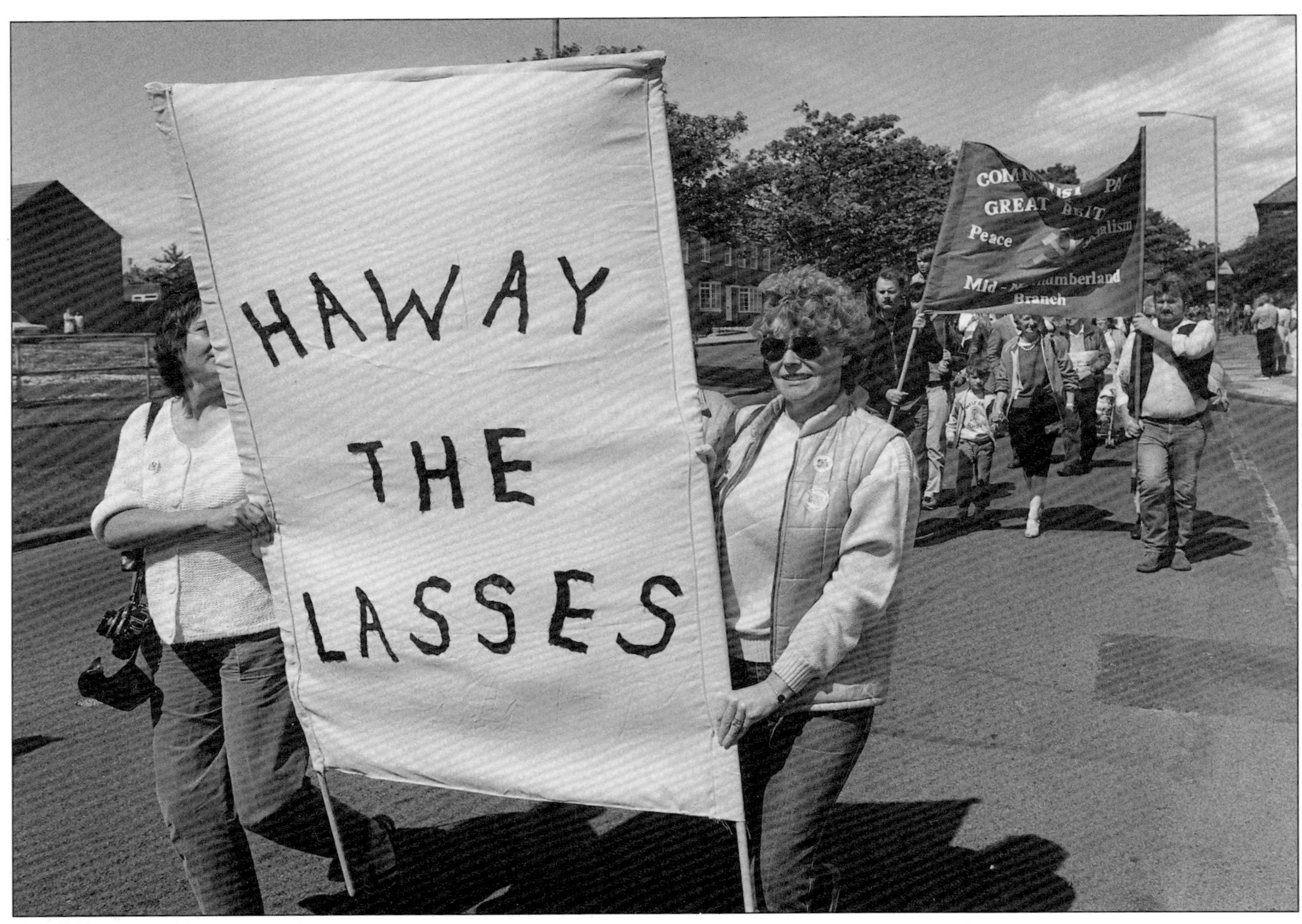


*Miners and their supporters marching near Ellington Colliery during the 1984-85 Miners' Strike*

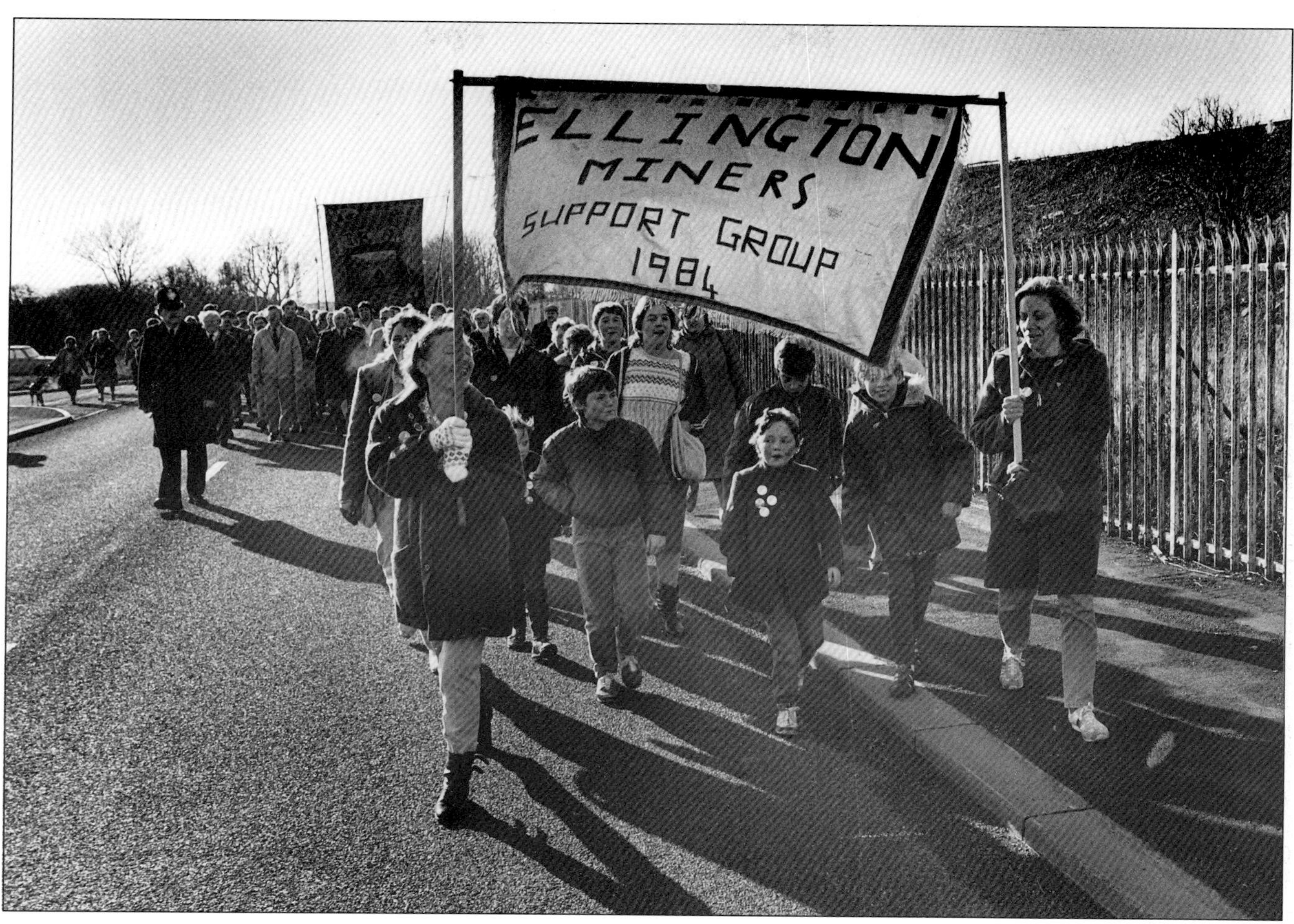


*Miners returning to work at the end of the strike, Ellington Colliery*

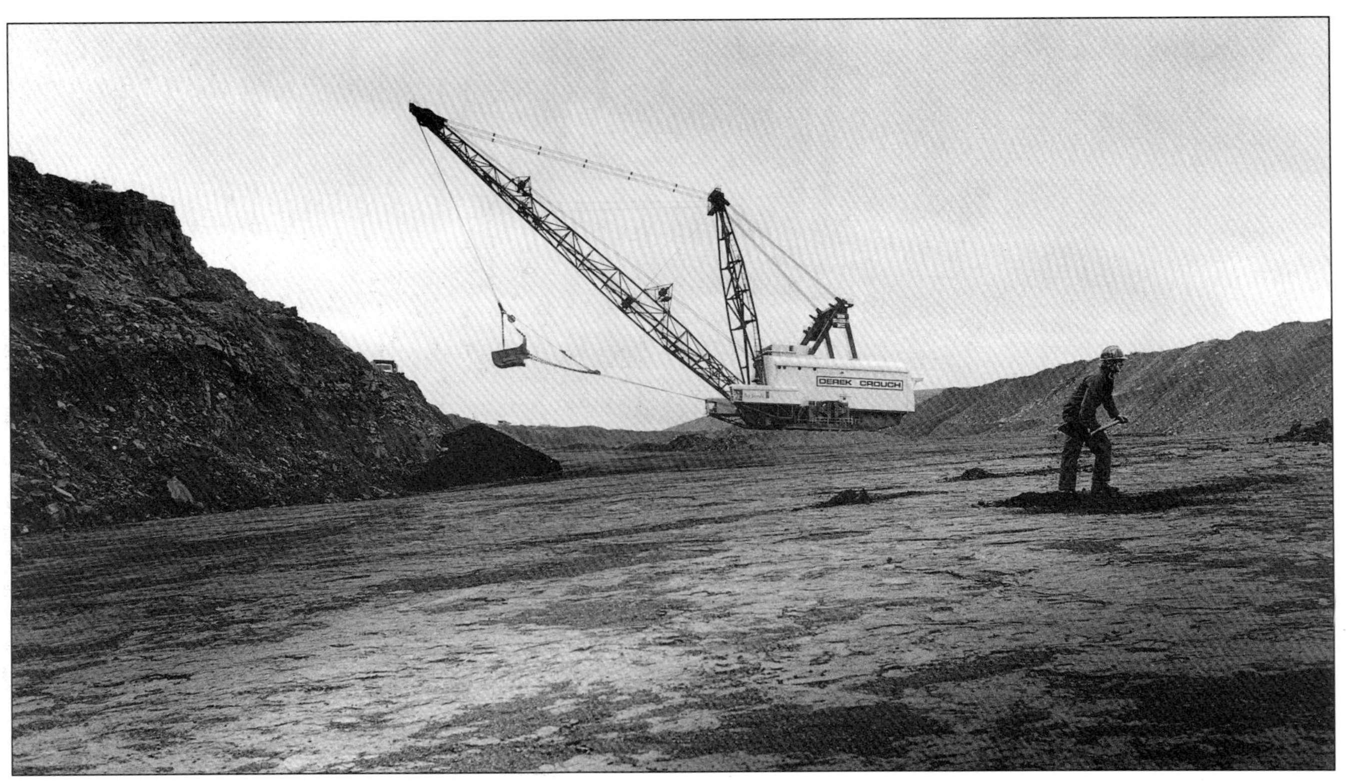


*The crane 'Big Geordie' at the Open Cast Coal Executive's mine at Butterwell, near Morpeth*

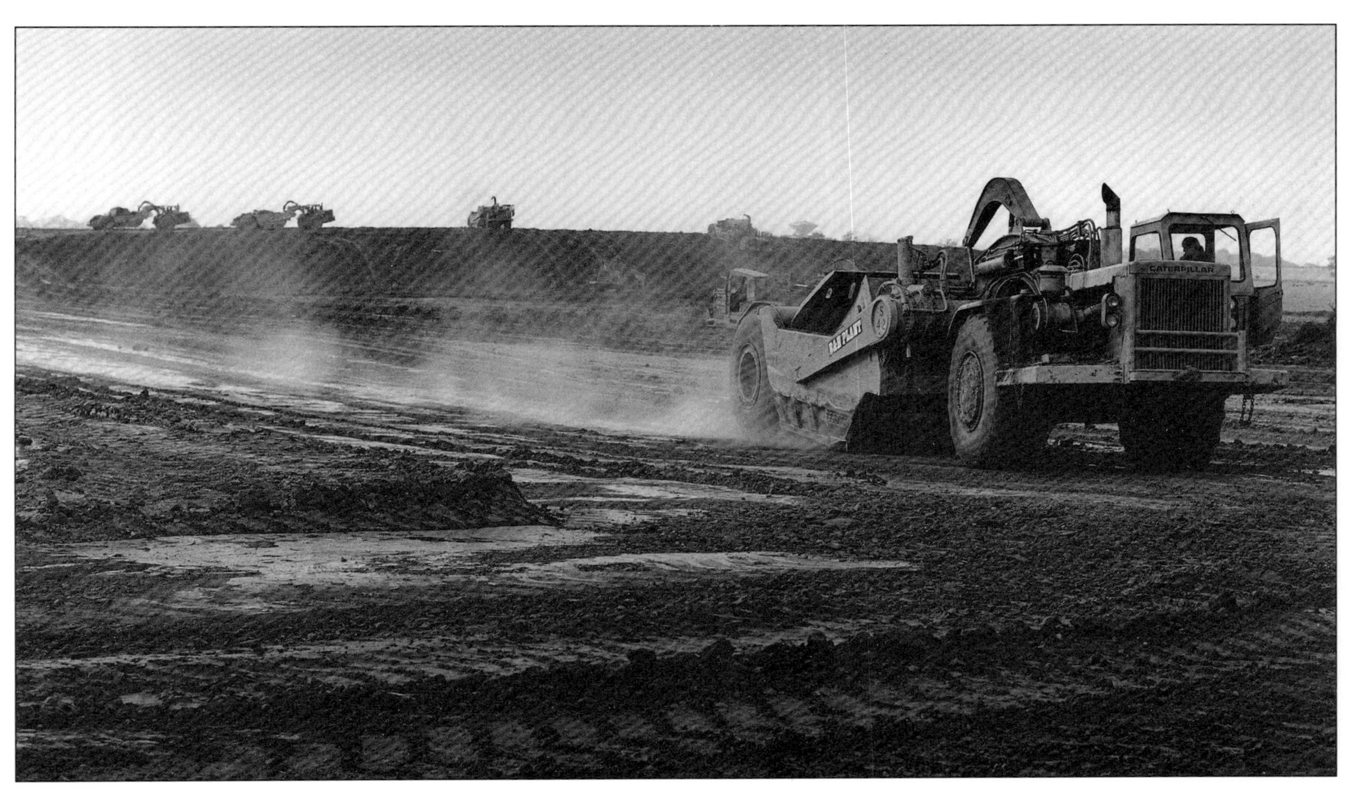


*Removal of soil and clay before open cast coal mining, near Warkworth*

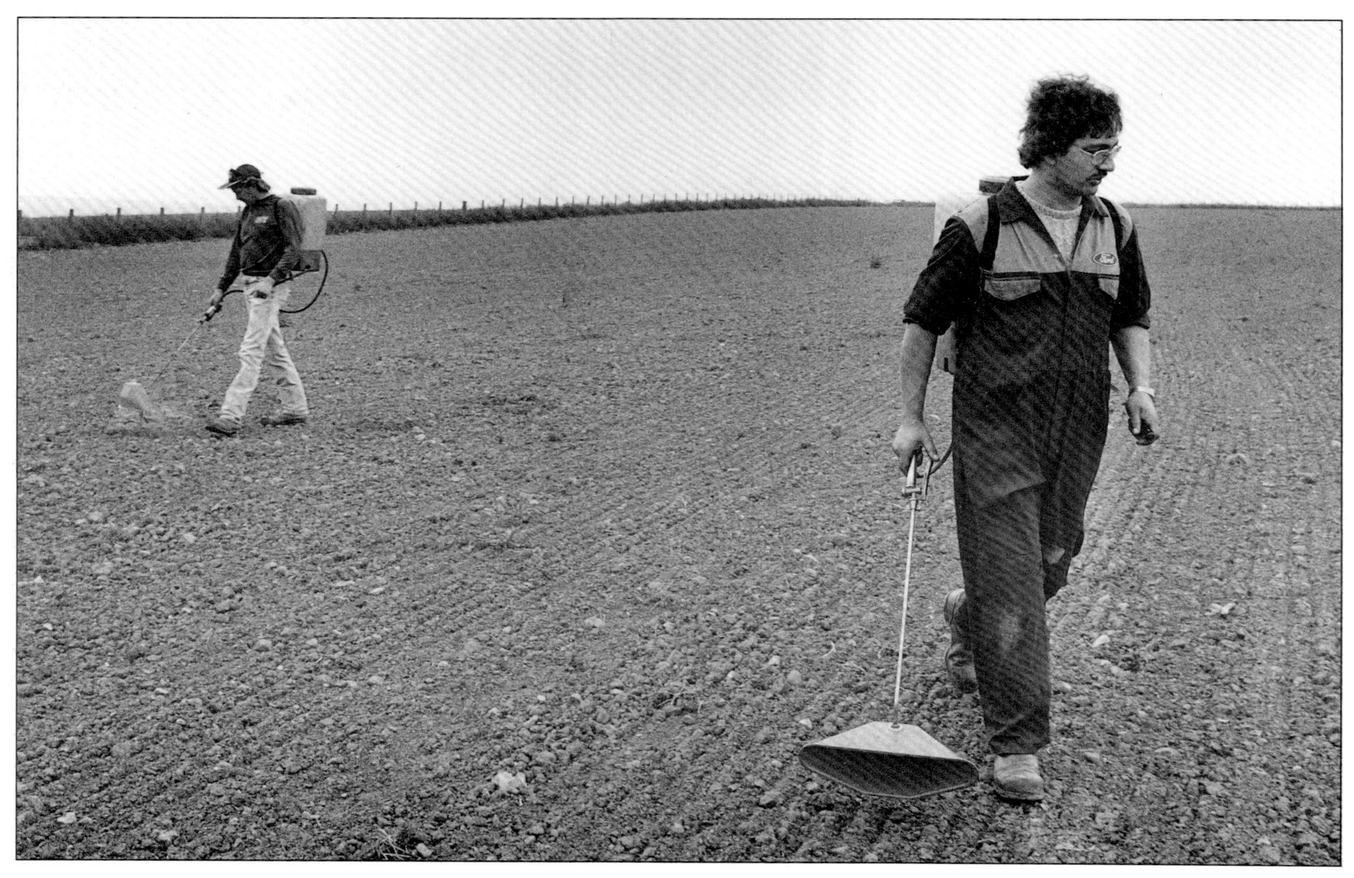

*Spraying docks on land recently returned to agriculture following open cast coal mining, near Morpeth*

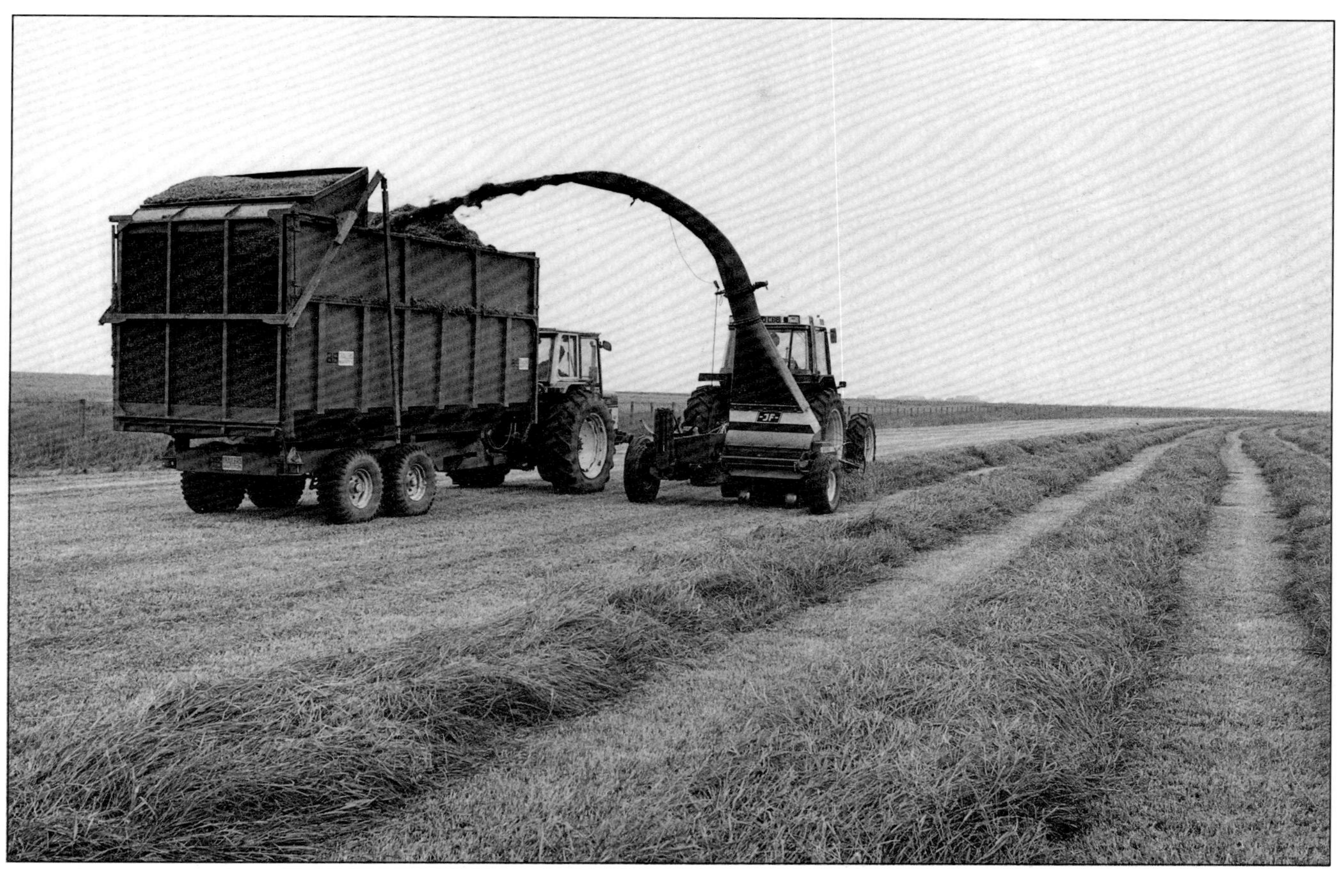

*Collecting hay on land returned to agriculture following open cast coal mining, near Widdrington*

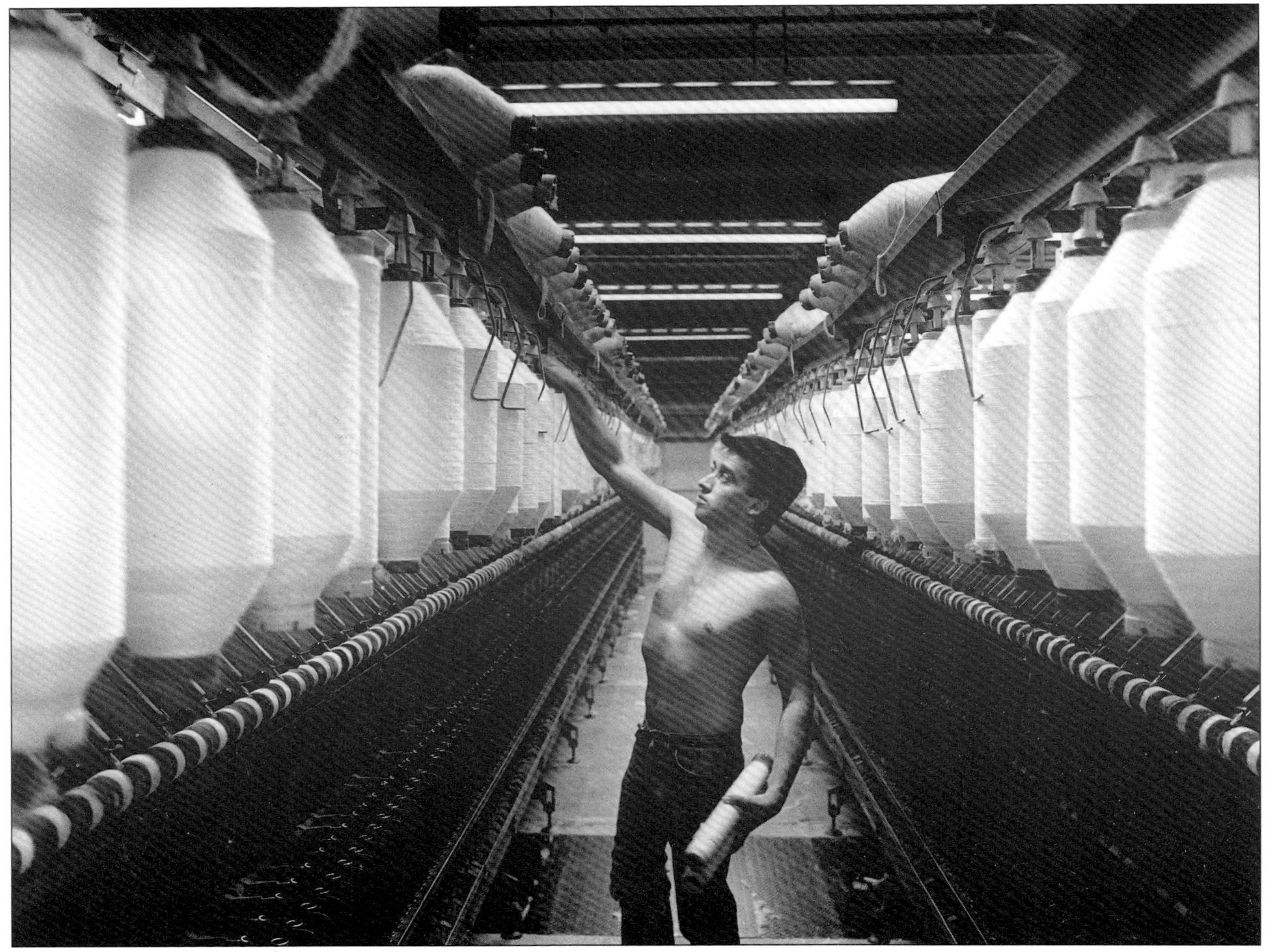

*Lonrho Textiles, Nelson Industrial Estate*

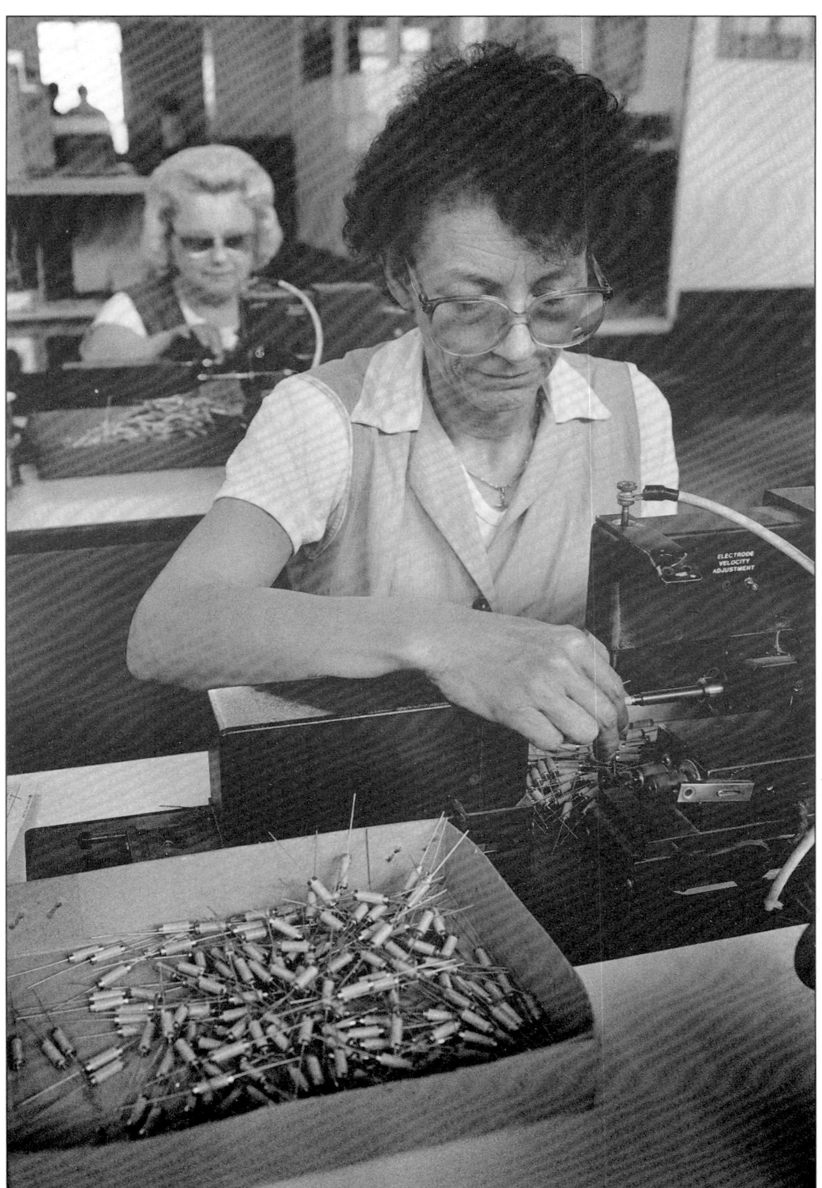


*Welwyn Electric,*
*Bedlington*

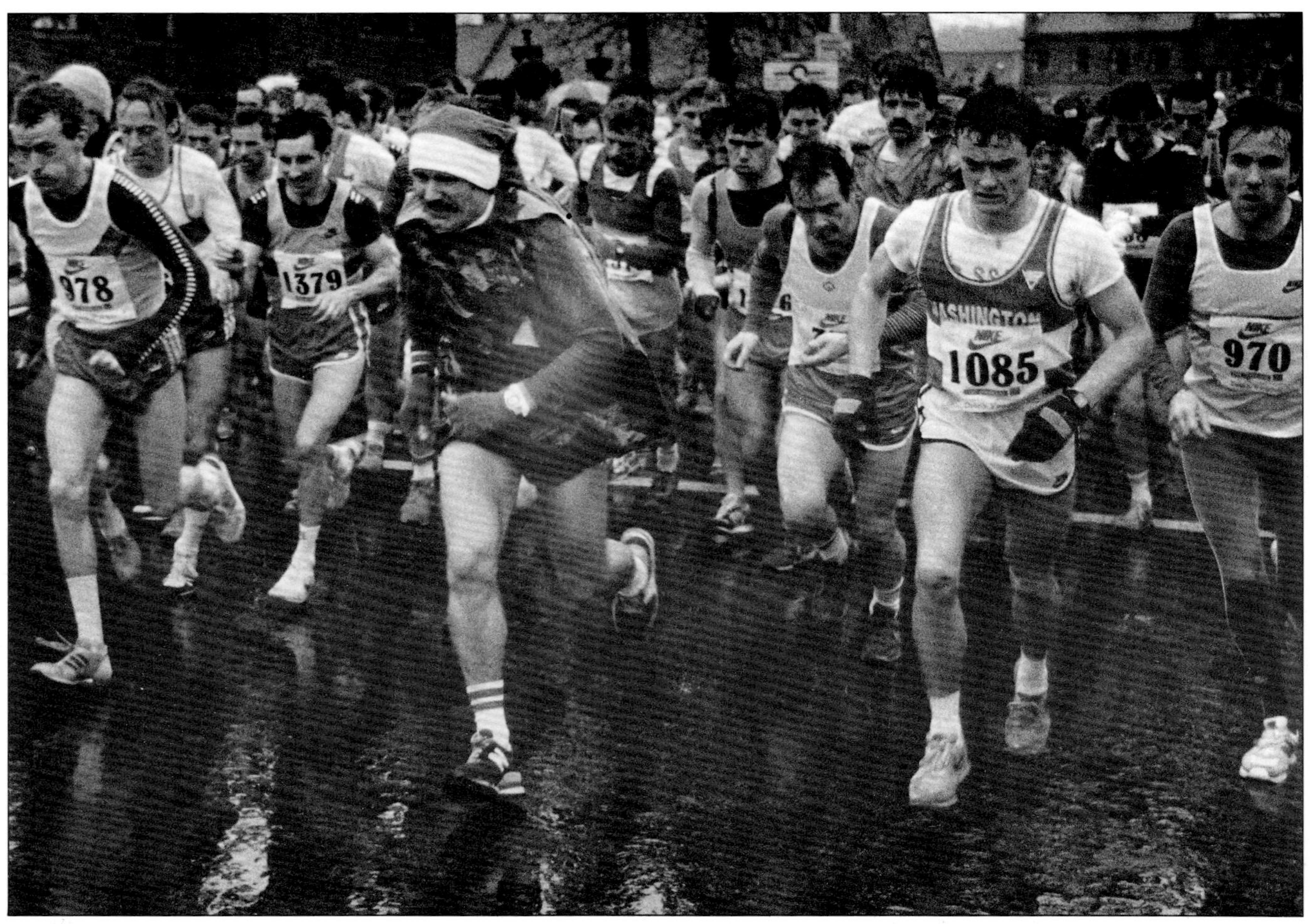


*The start of the Morpeth to Newcastle road race, held every new year's day*

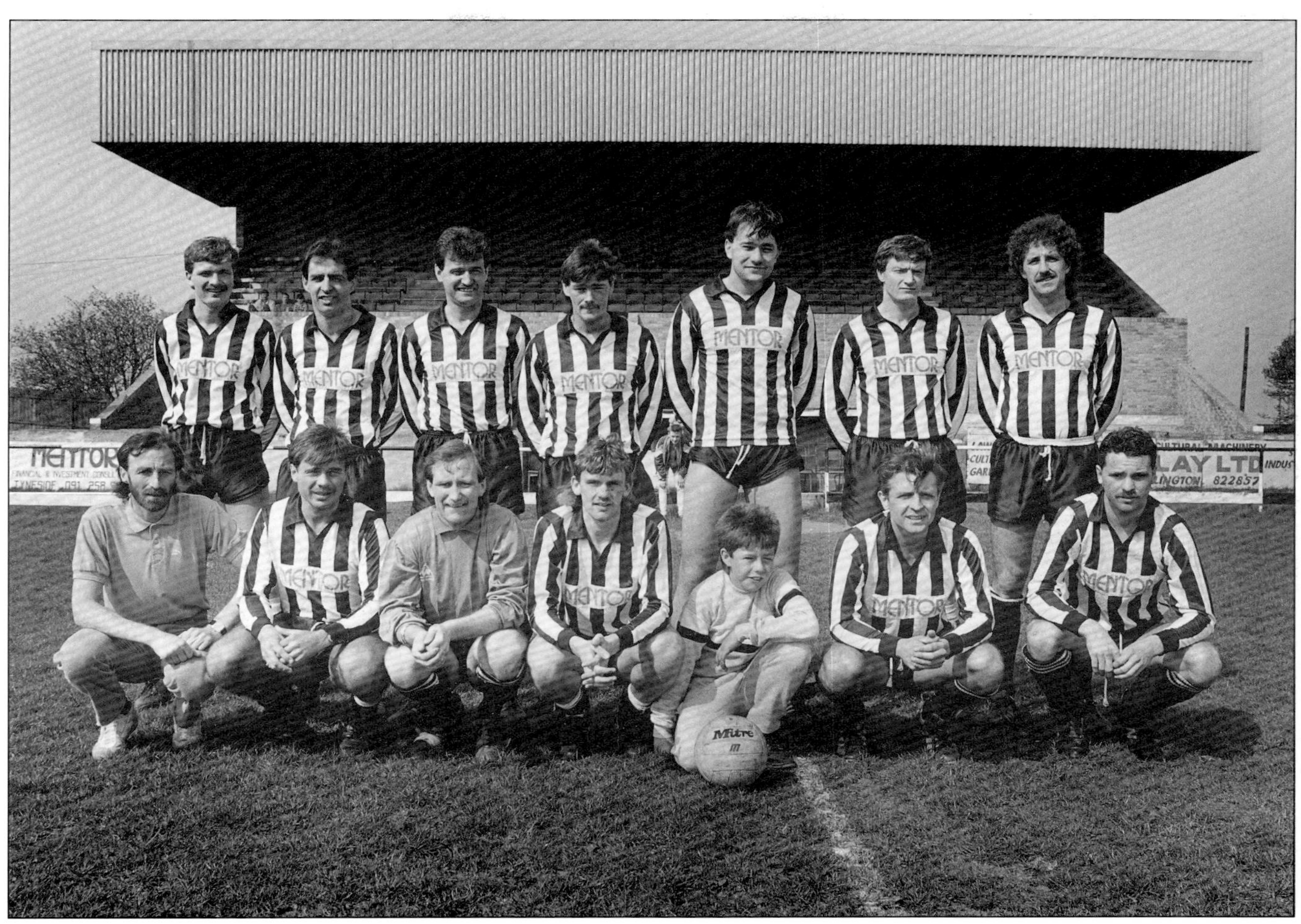


*Ashington football team*

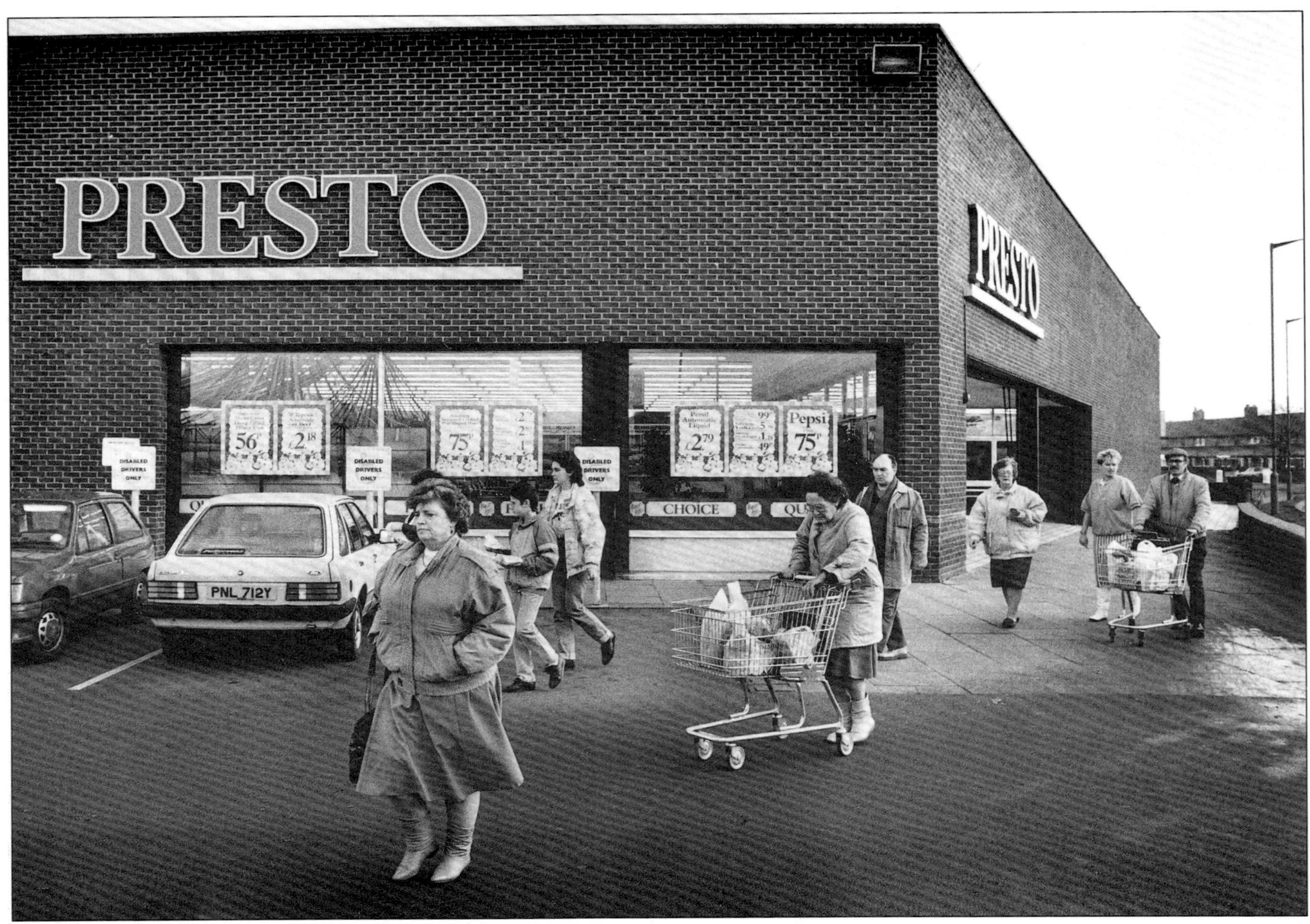


*Supermarket, Ashington*

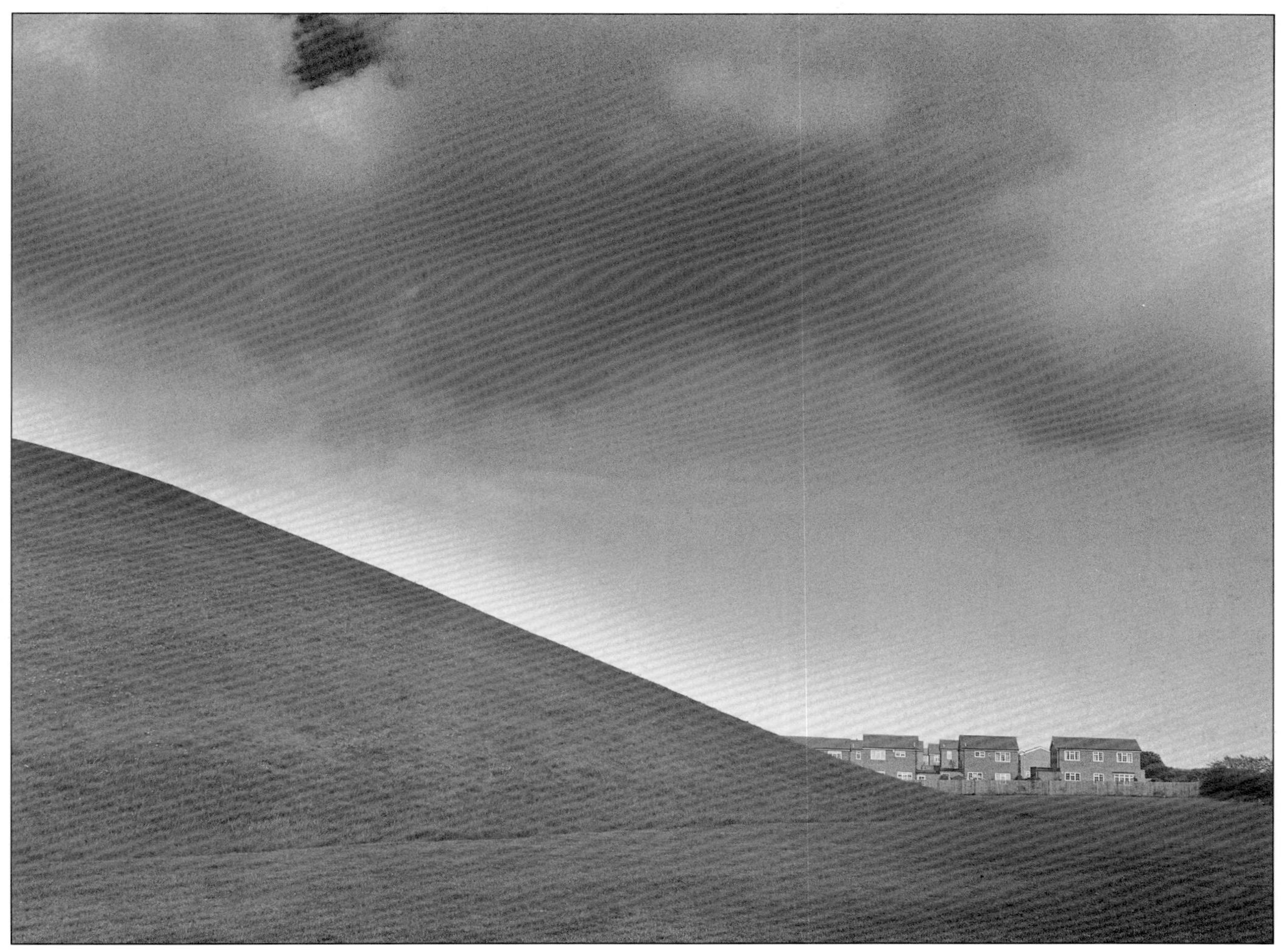

*Housing estate, Cramlington, below a reclaimed pit heap*

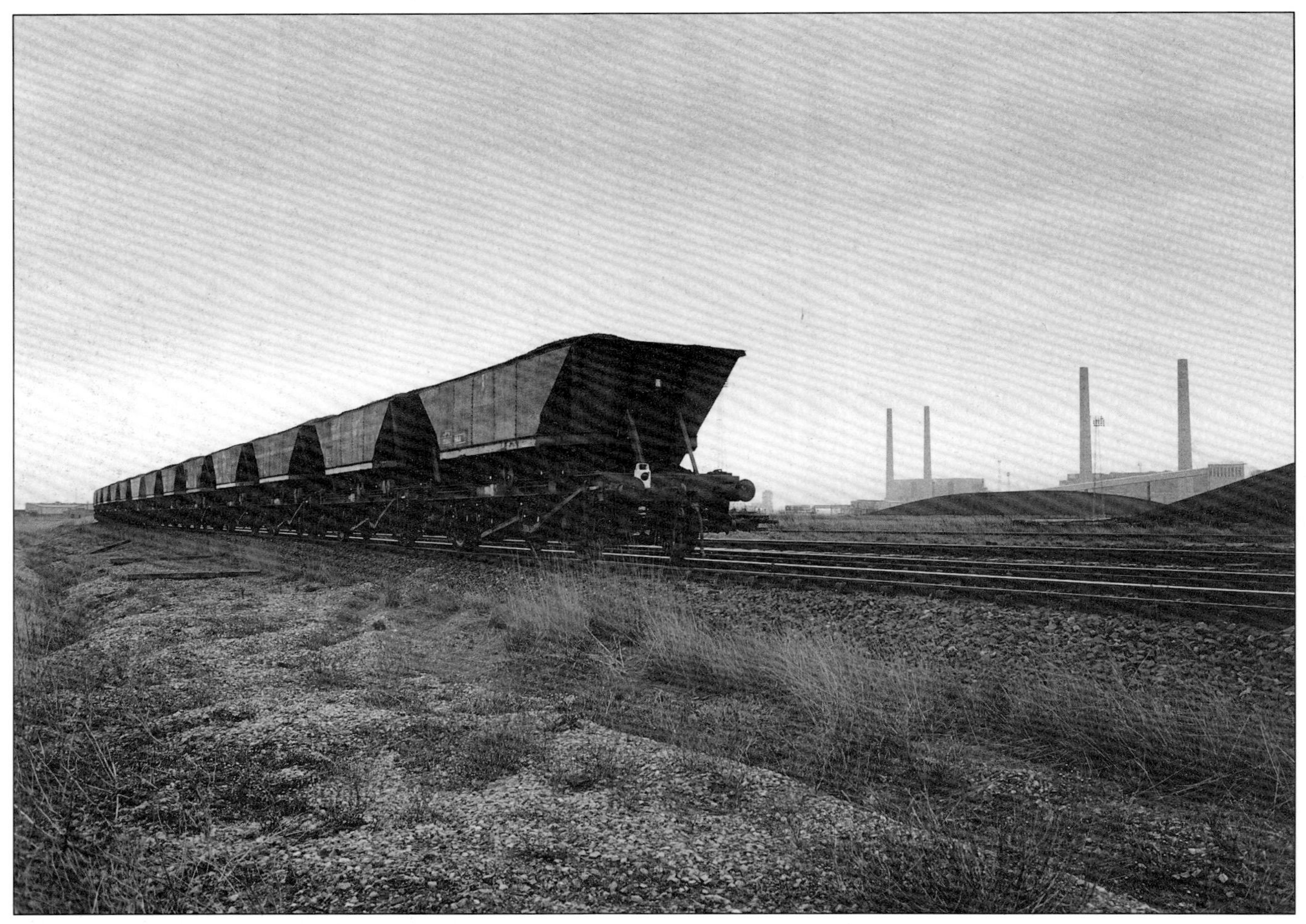

*Blyth Power Station*

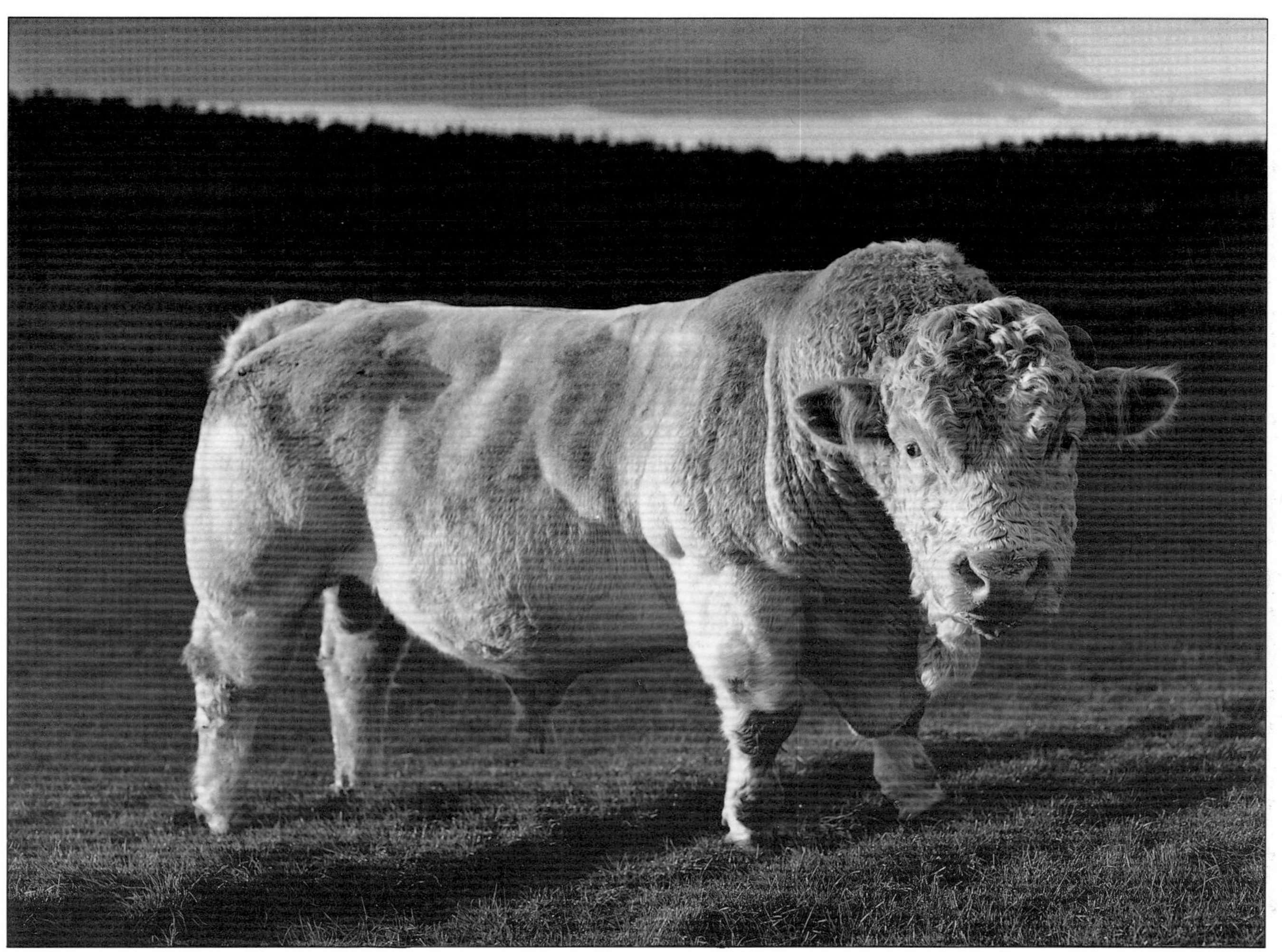

*Charolais bull, New Bewick Farm, near Alnwick*

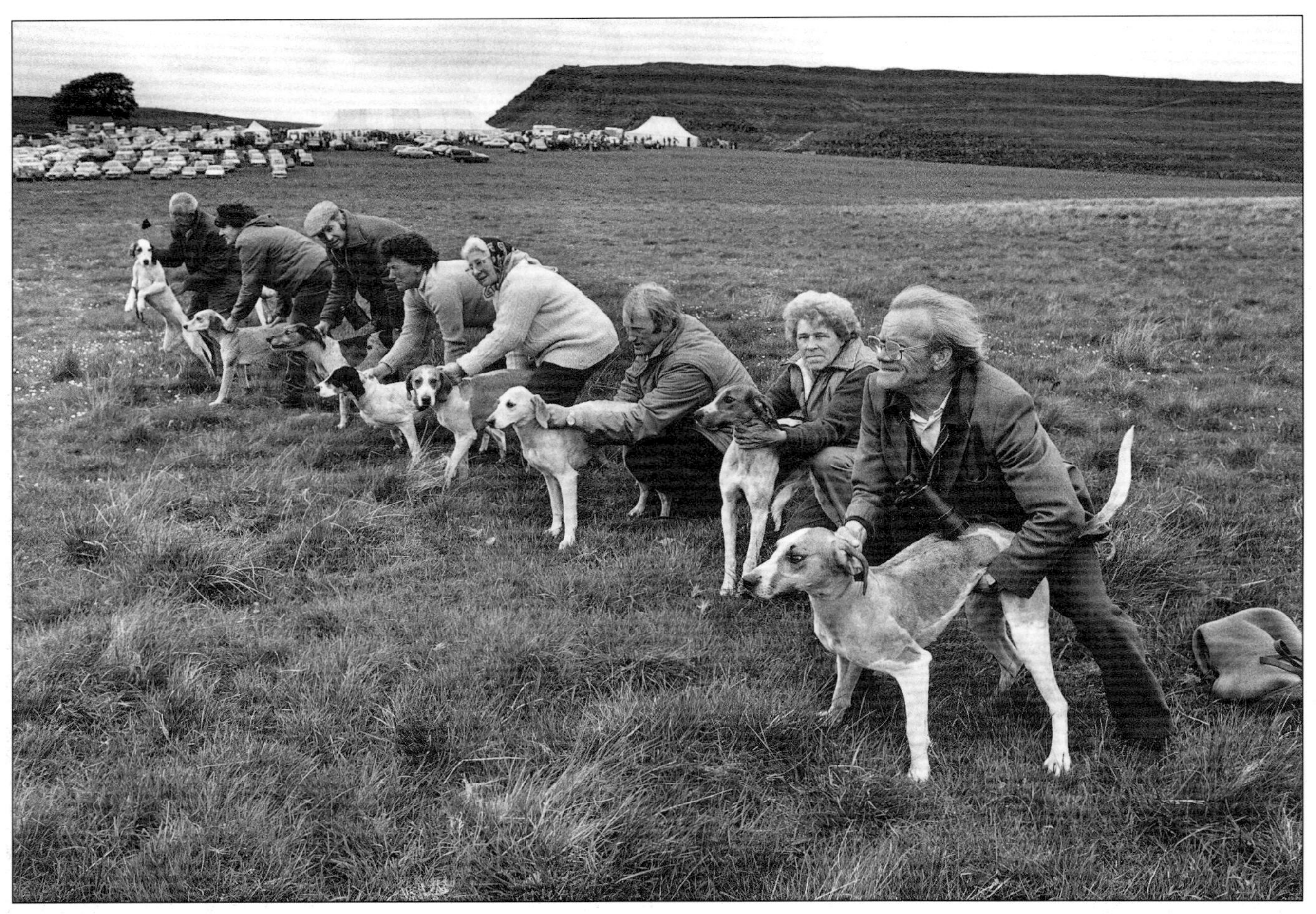

*The Roman Wall Show, near Twice Brewed*

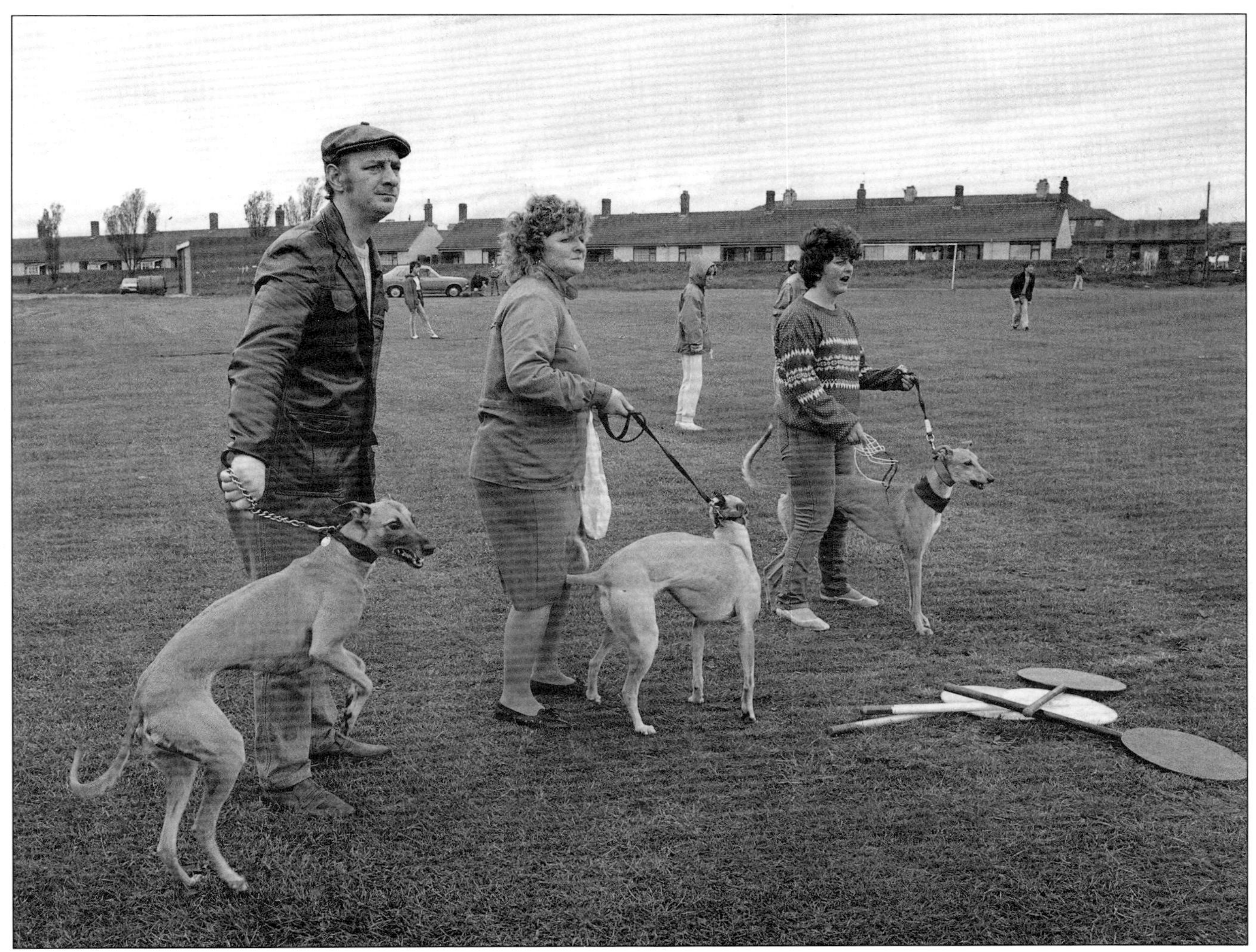

*Whippet race meeting, Hirst Park, Ashington*

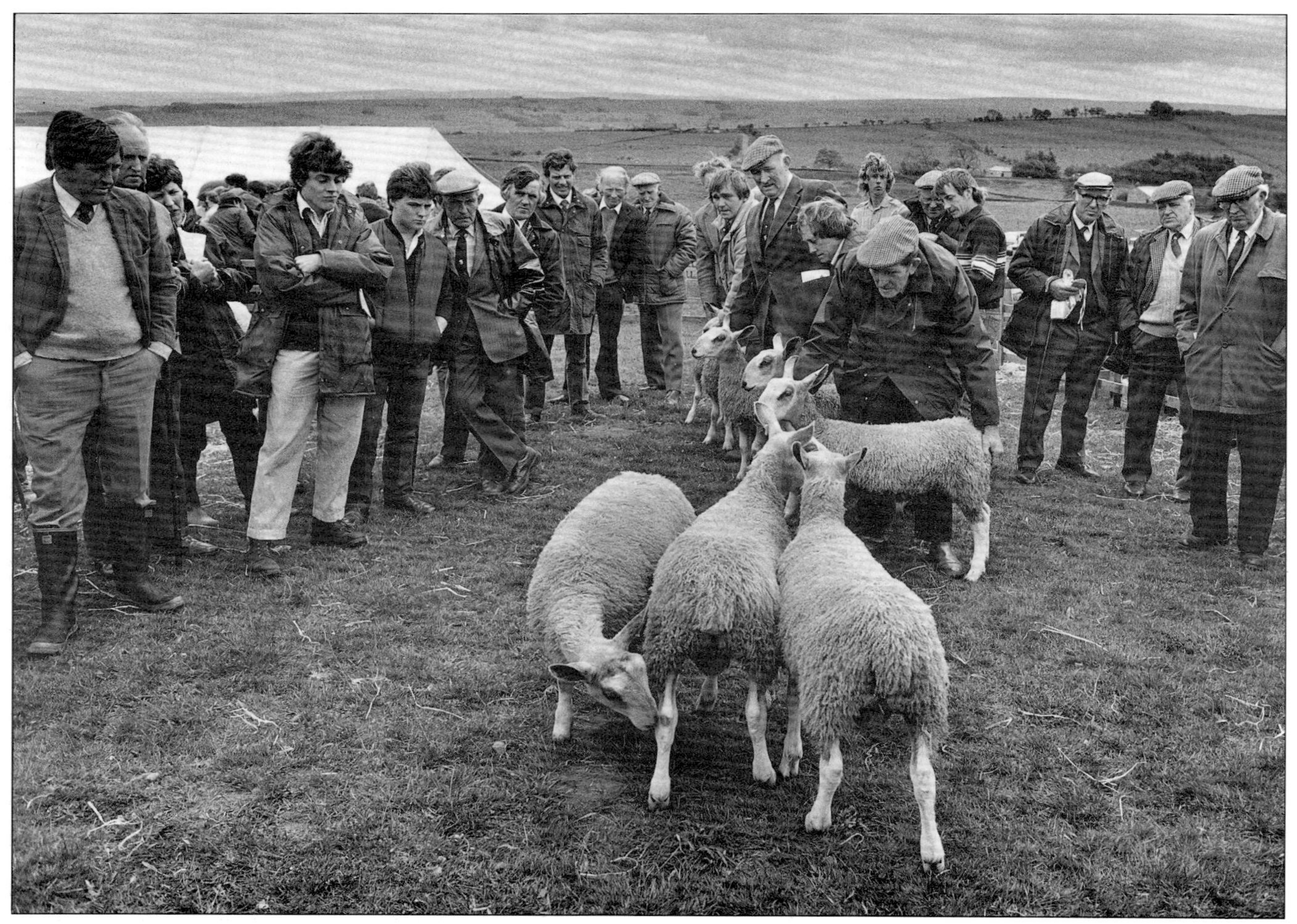

*The Roman Wall Show, near Twice Brewed*

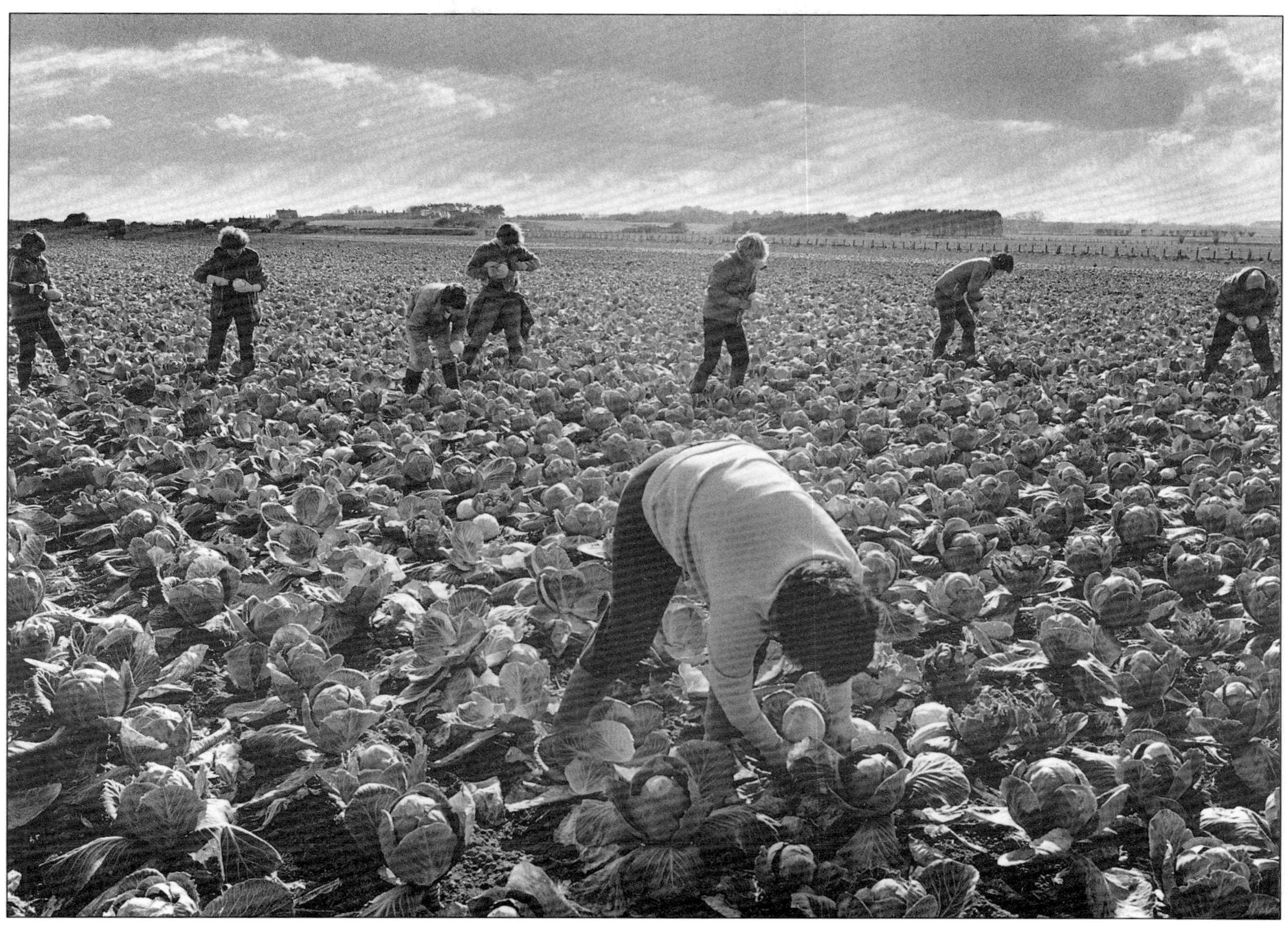

*Harvesting cabbages, Field House Farm, near Lesbury*

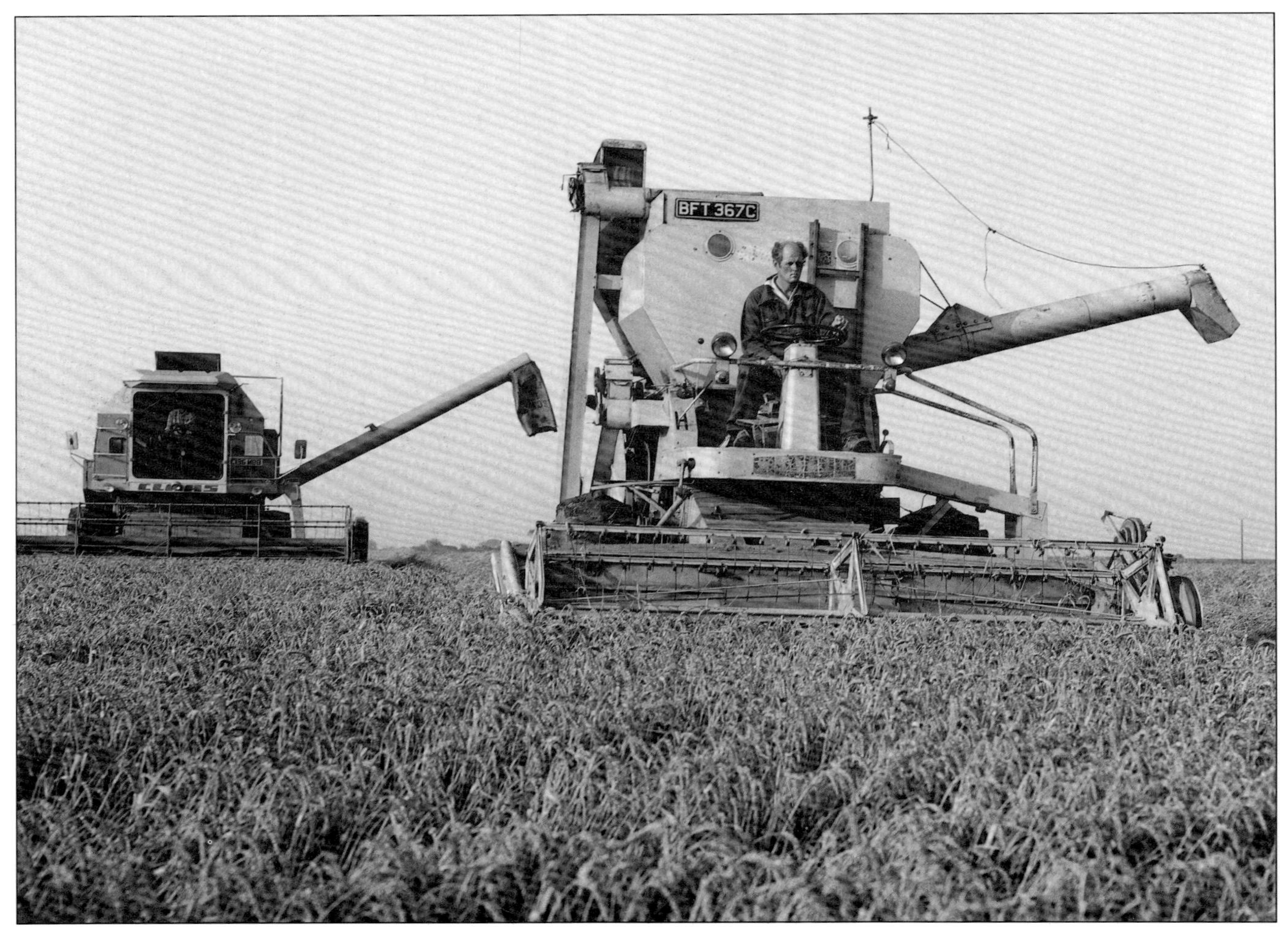


*Combine harvesting, Buston Barns Farm, near Warkworth*

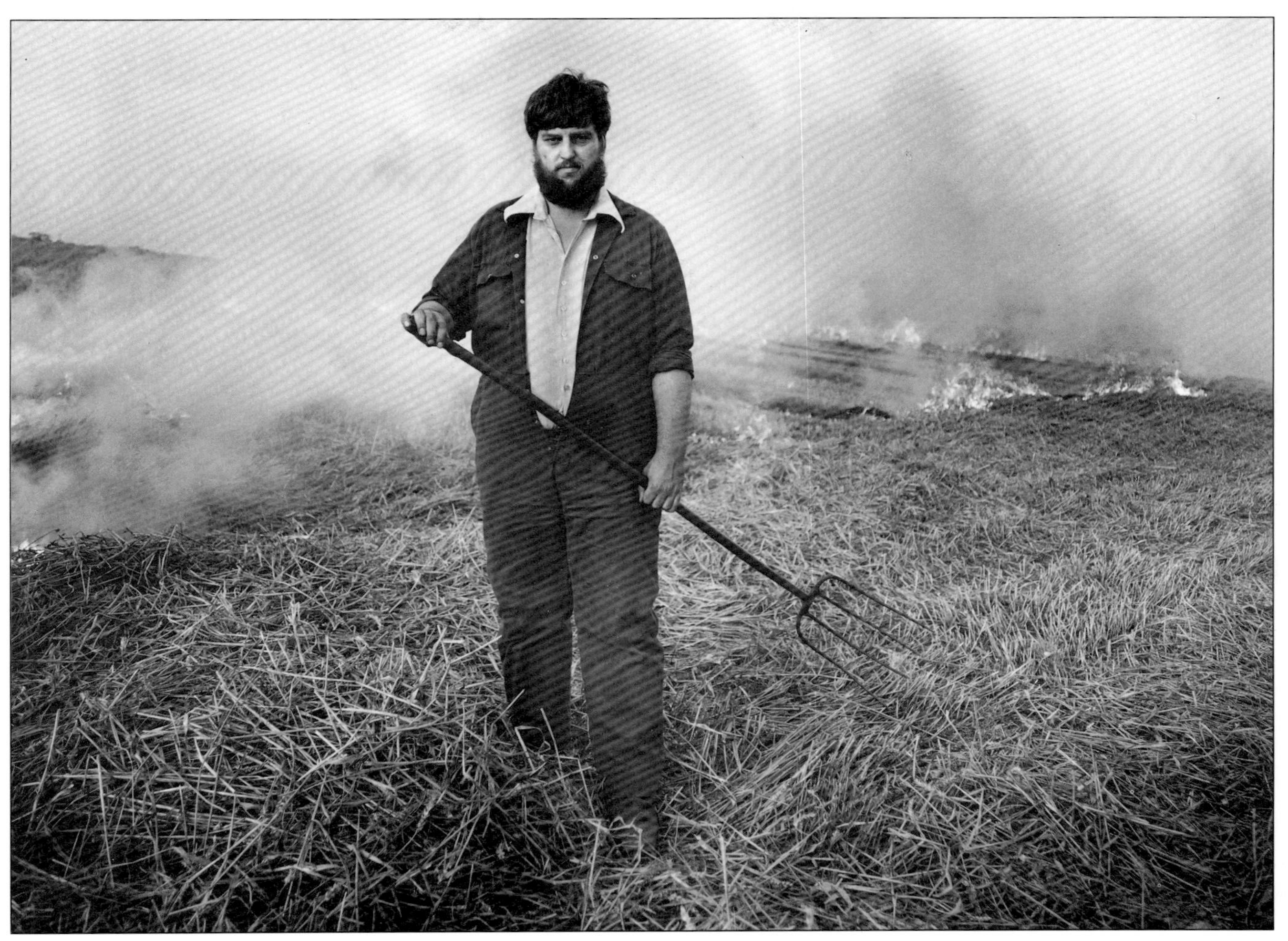

*Straw-burning following harvesting, Buston Barns Farm*

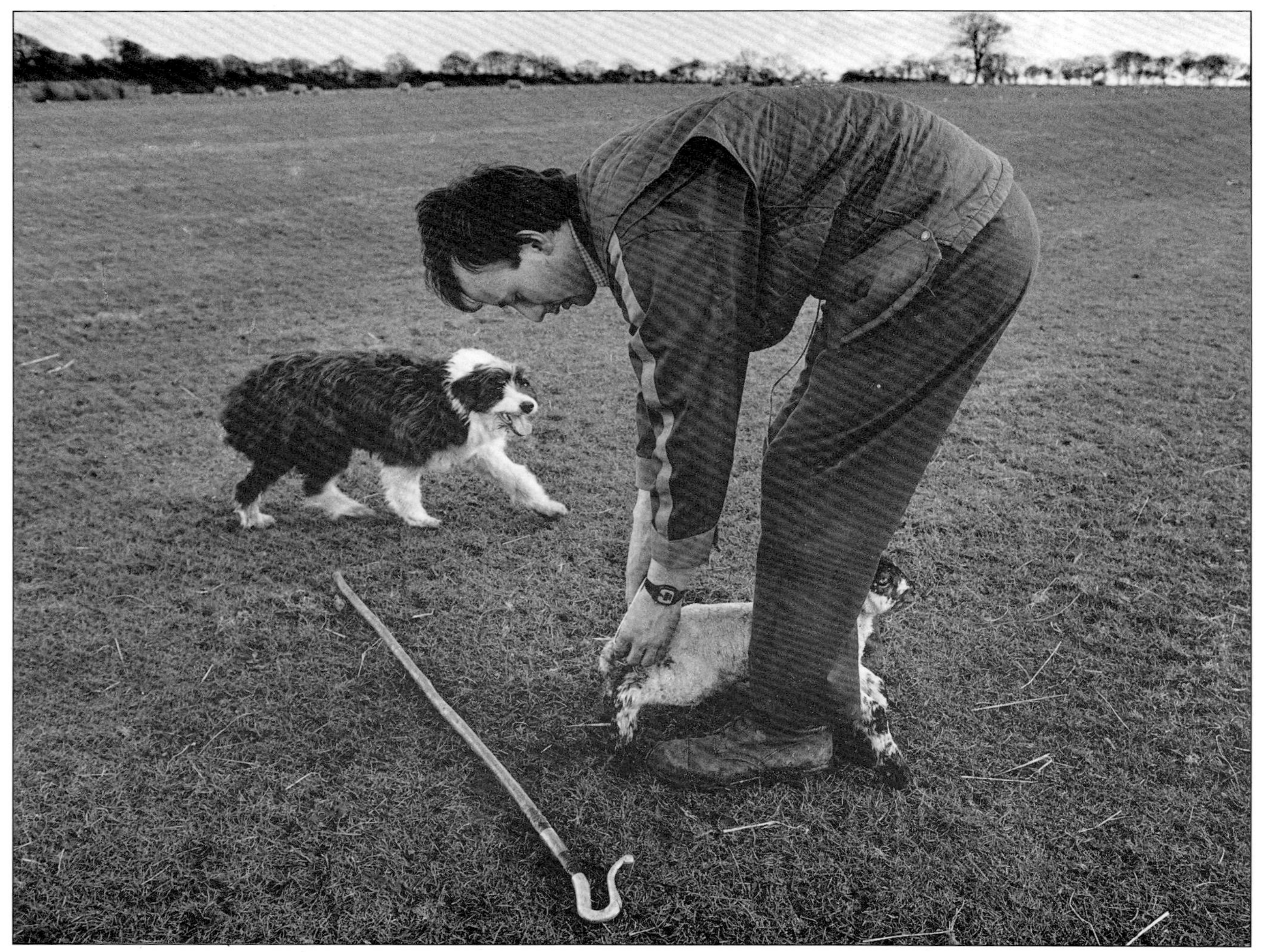

*Docking a lamb's tail, Red Stead Farm, near Howick*

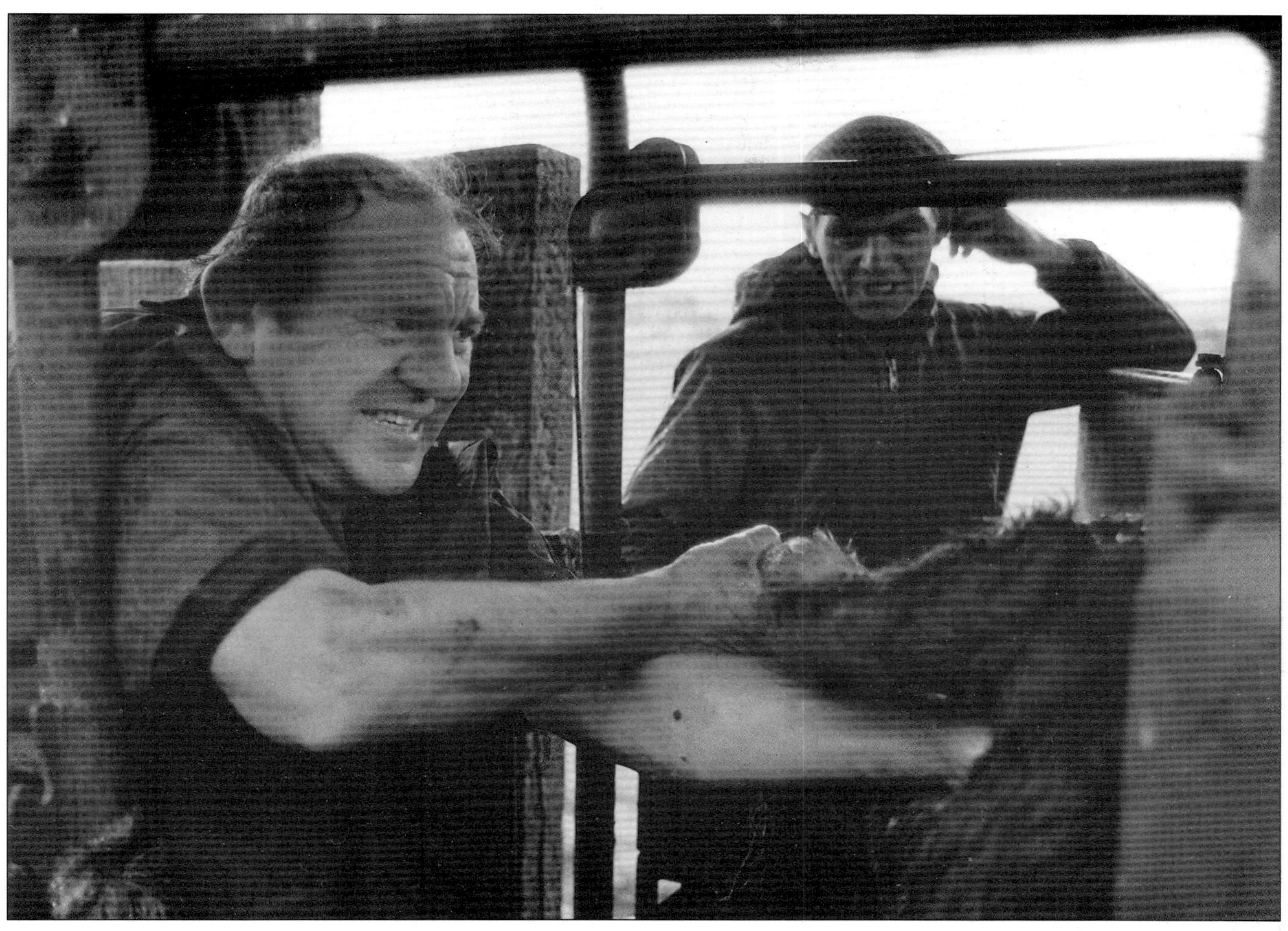

*Bruce Robson, a Morpeth vet at Shaftoe Grange, near Belsay*

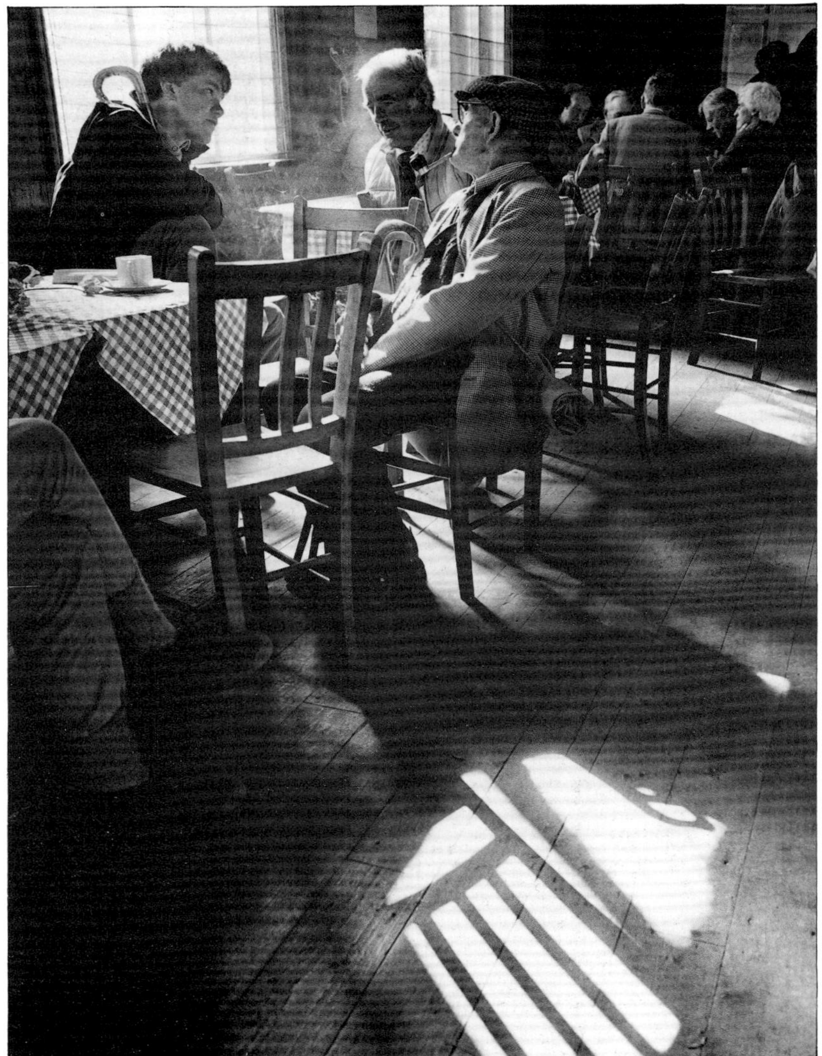

*The village tea-room during the Ingram Show*

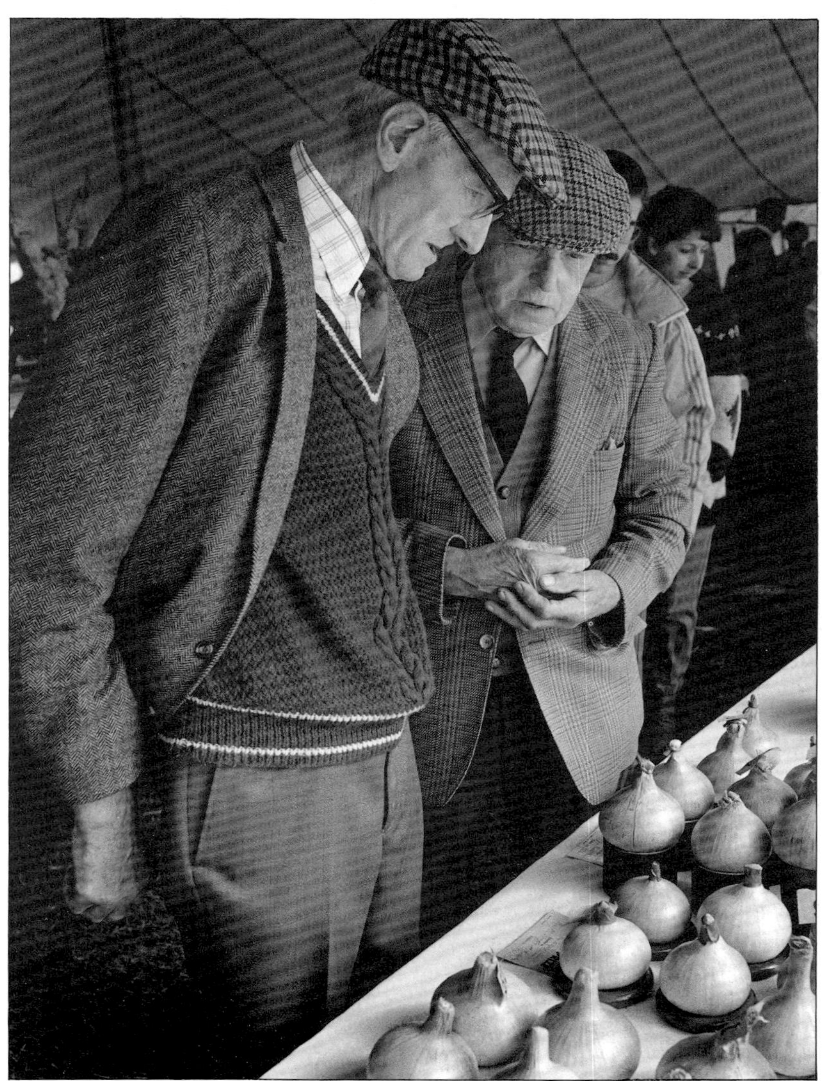

*Thropton Agricultural Show*

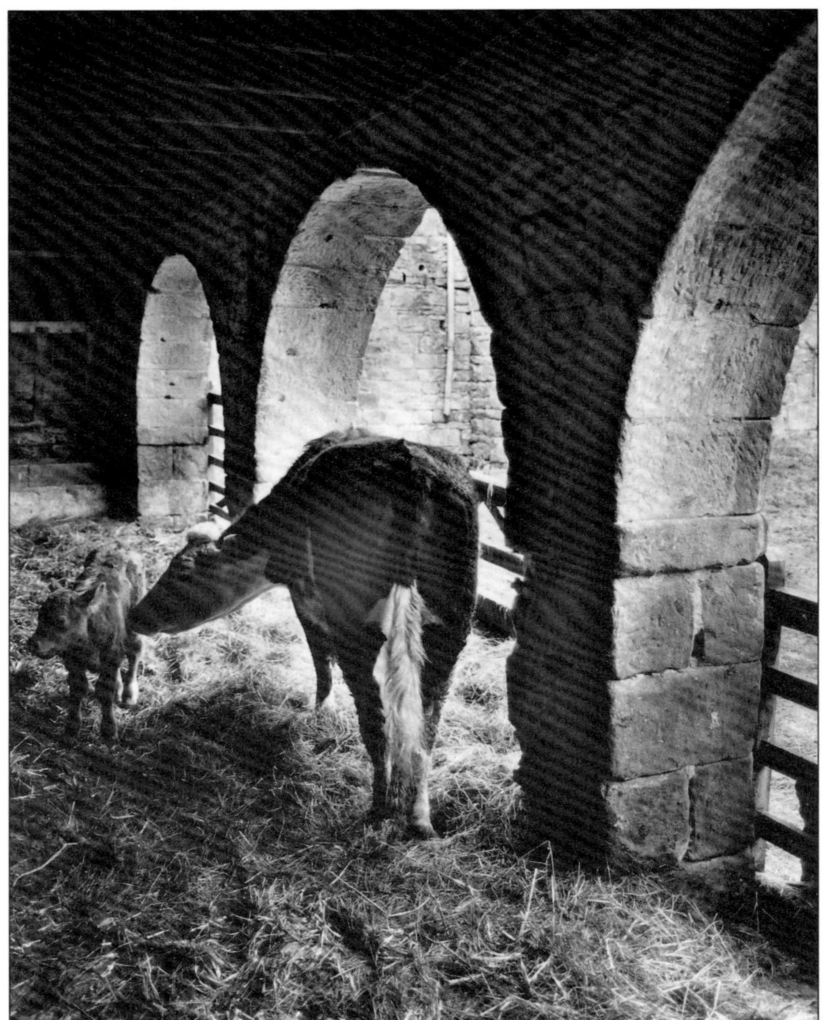

*A byre at Rochester, near Otterburn*

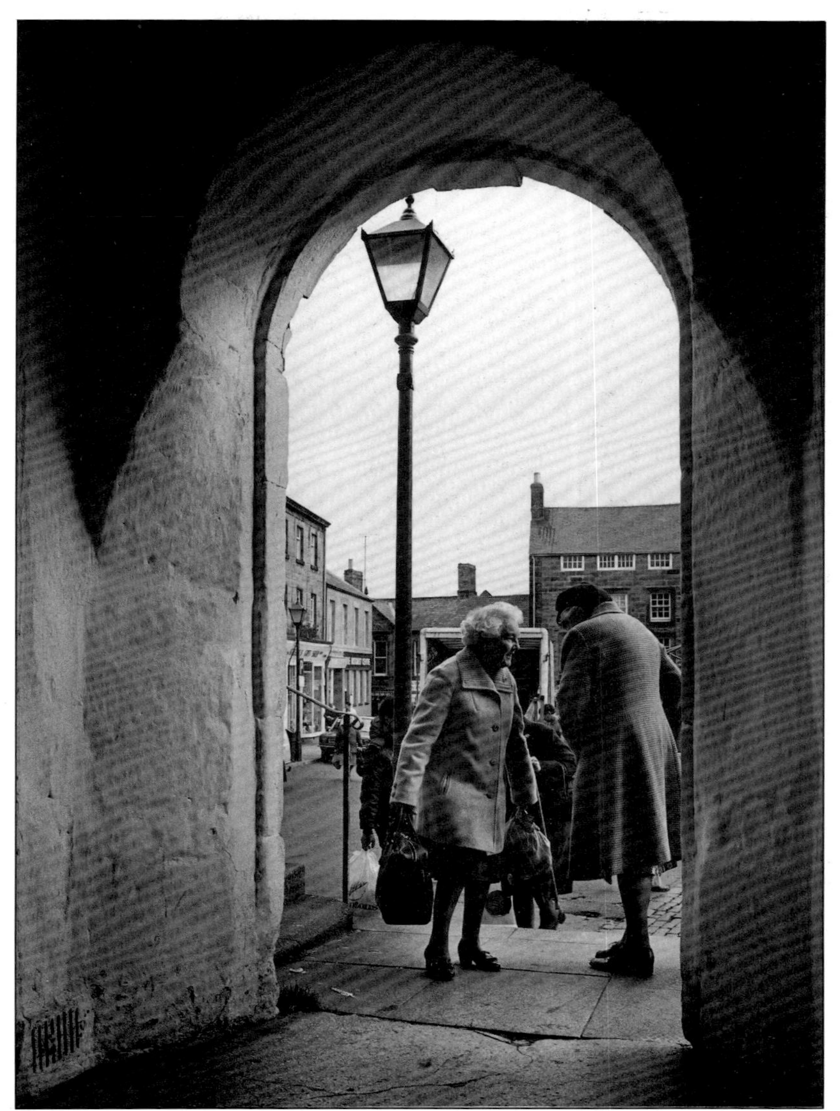

*By the Market Place, Alnwick*

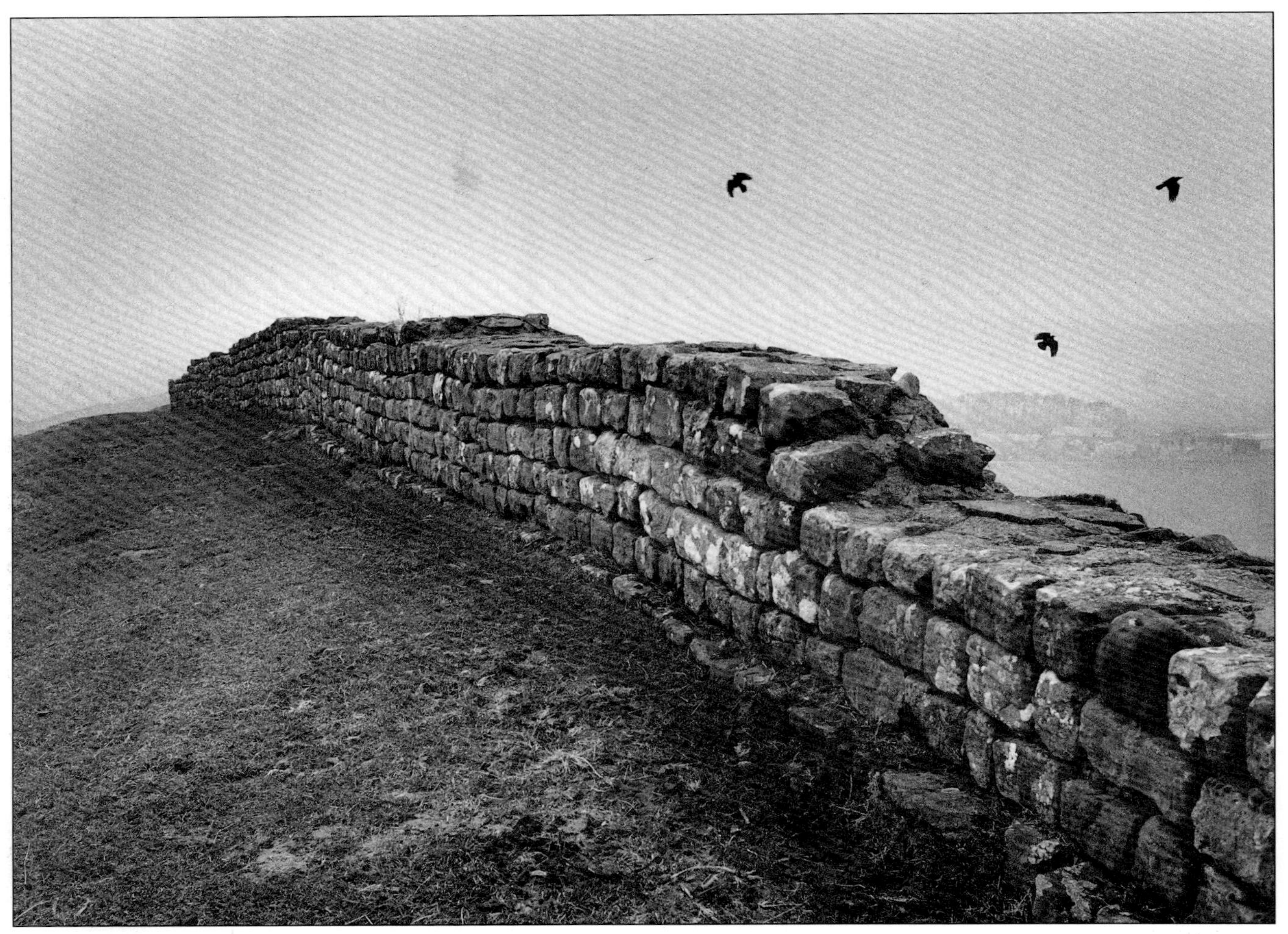

*Hadrian's Wall above Cawfield Crags*

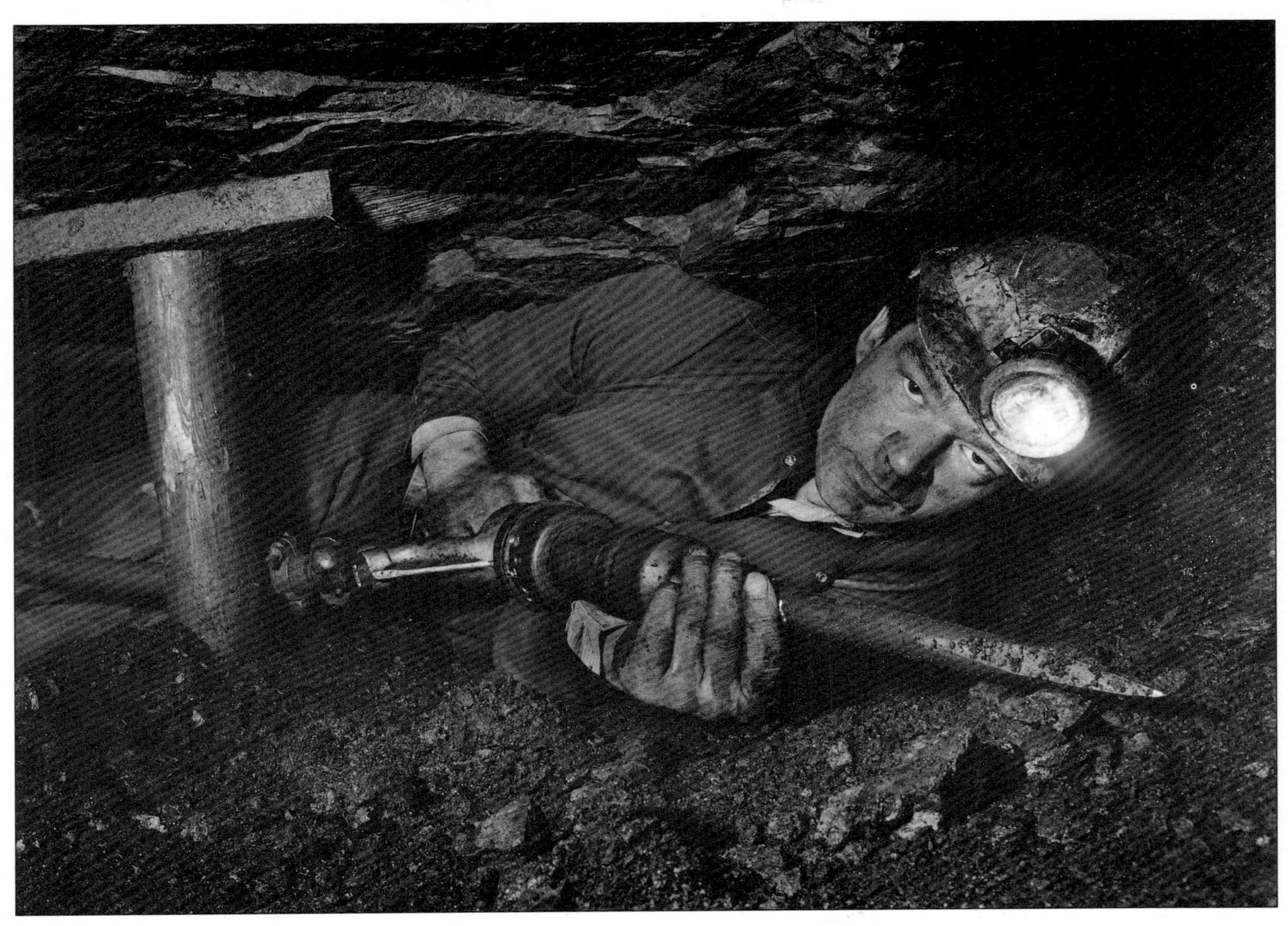

*A private coal-mine near Coanwood*

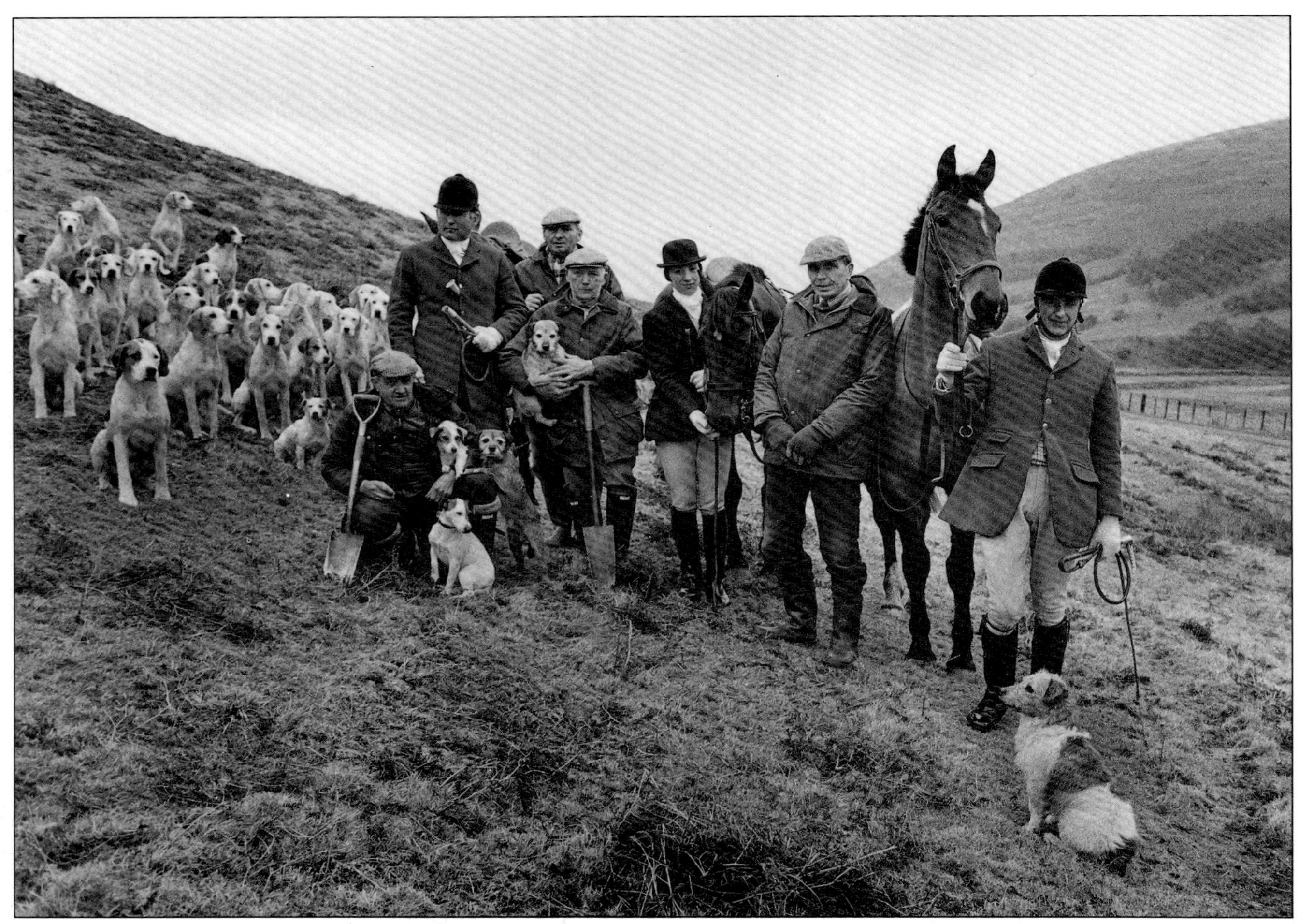

*The College Valley Hunt*

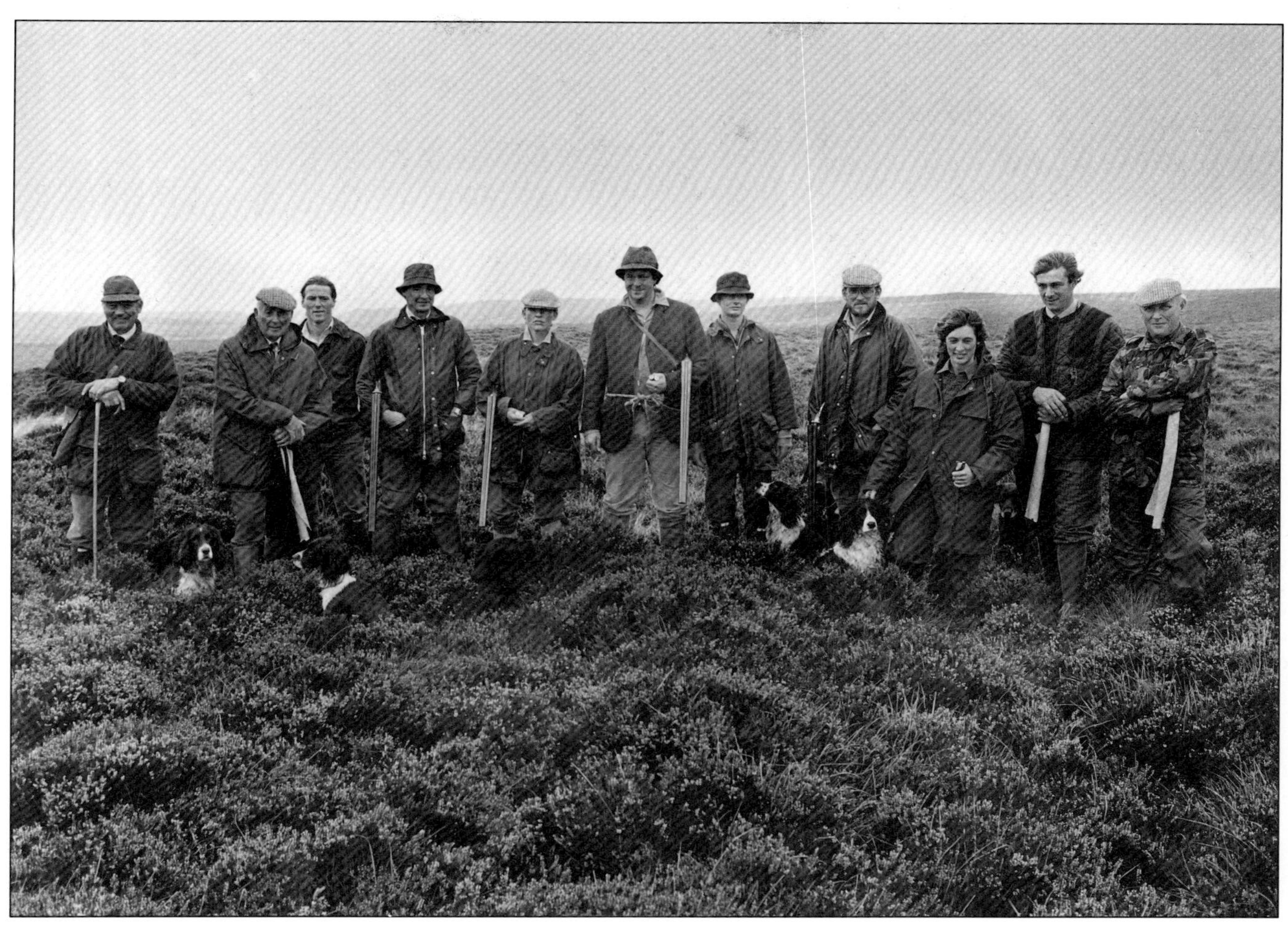

*A shooting party on Lord Redesdale's estate, near Kirkwhelpington*

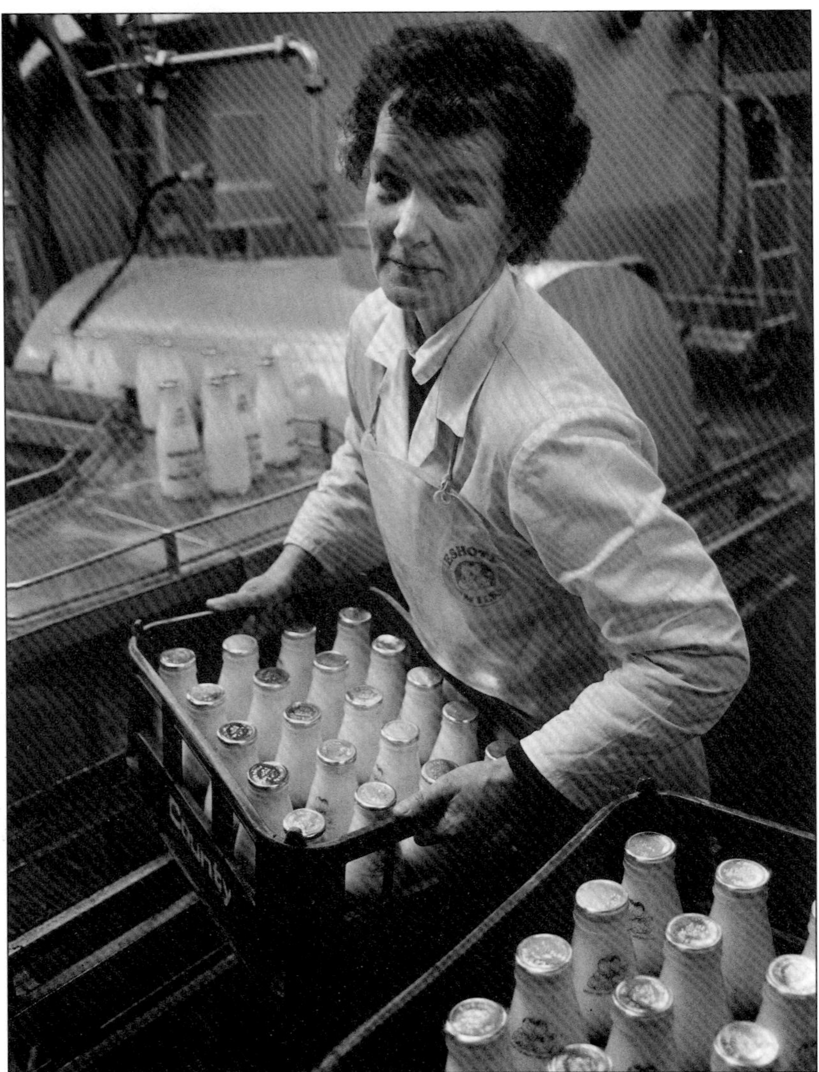


*Eshott Dairy*

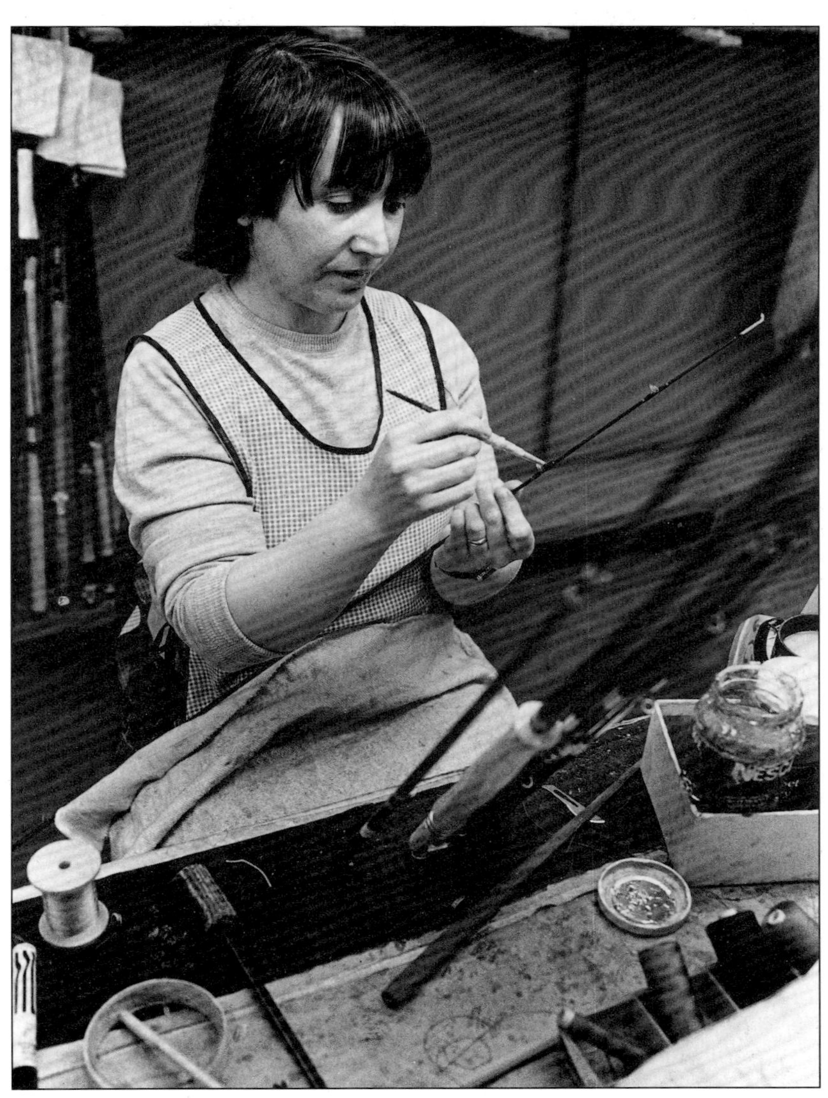

*Hardy's, fishing tackle makers, Alnwick*

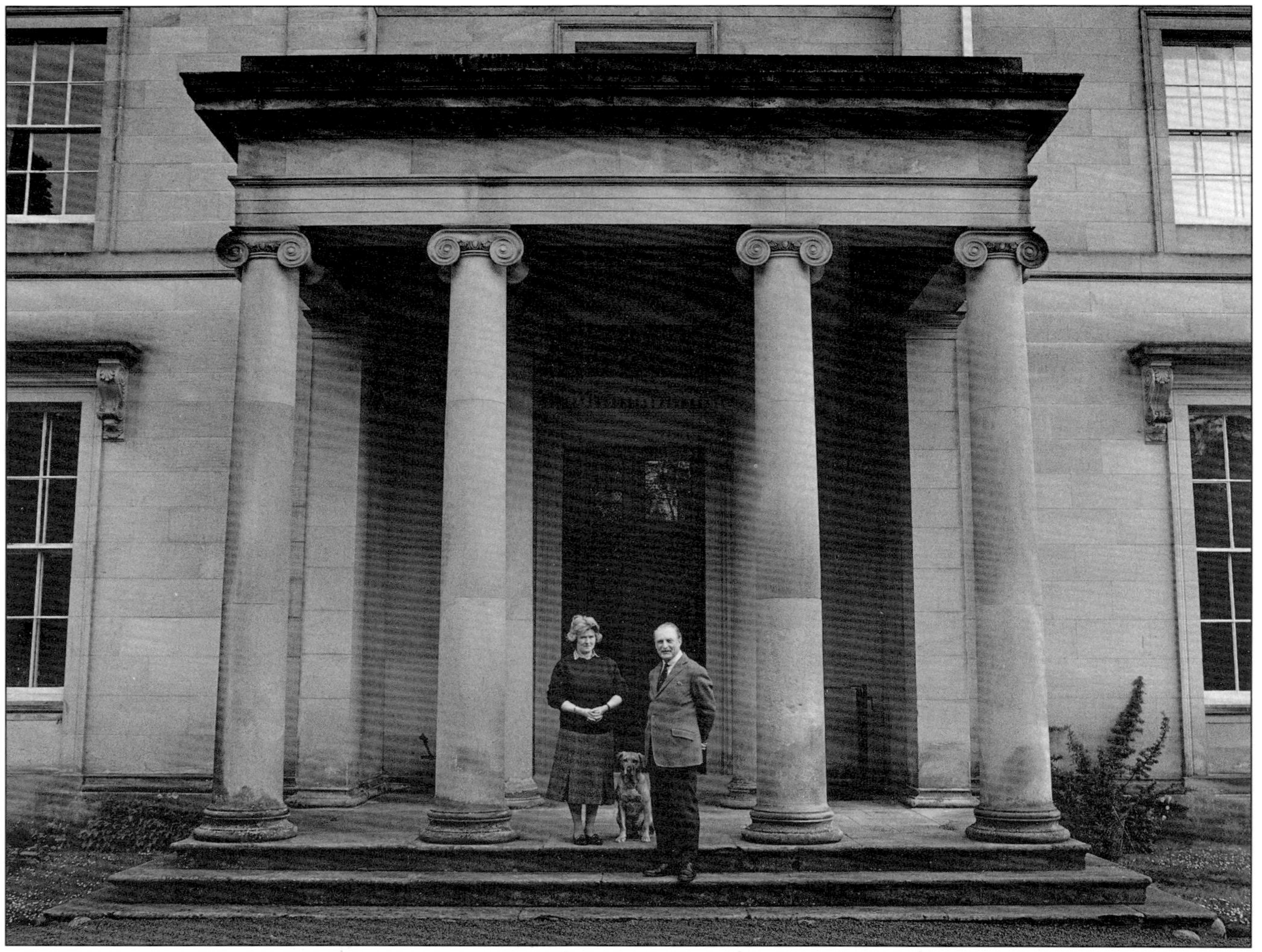

*The Cooksons of Meldon Hall, near Mitford*

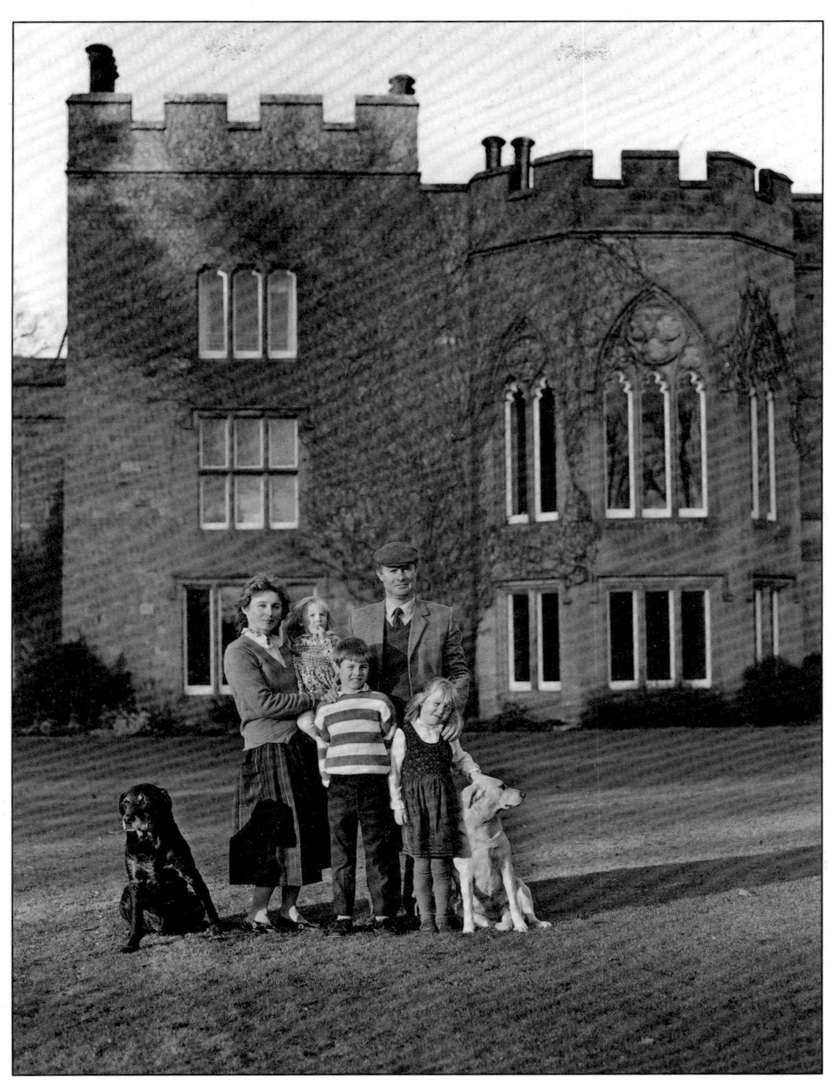

*The Anderson family, Littleharle Tower, near Wallington*

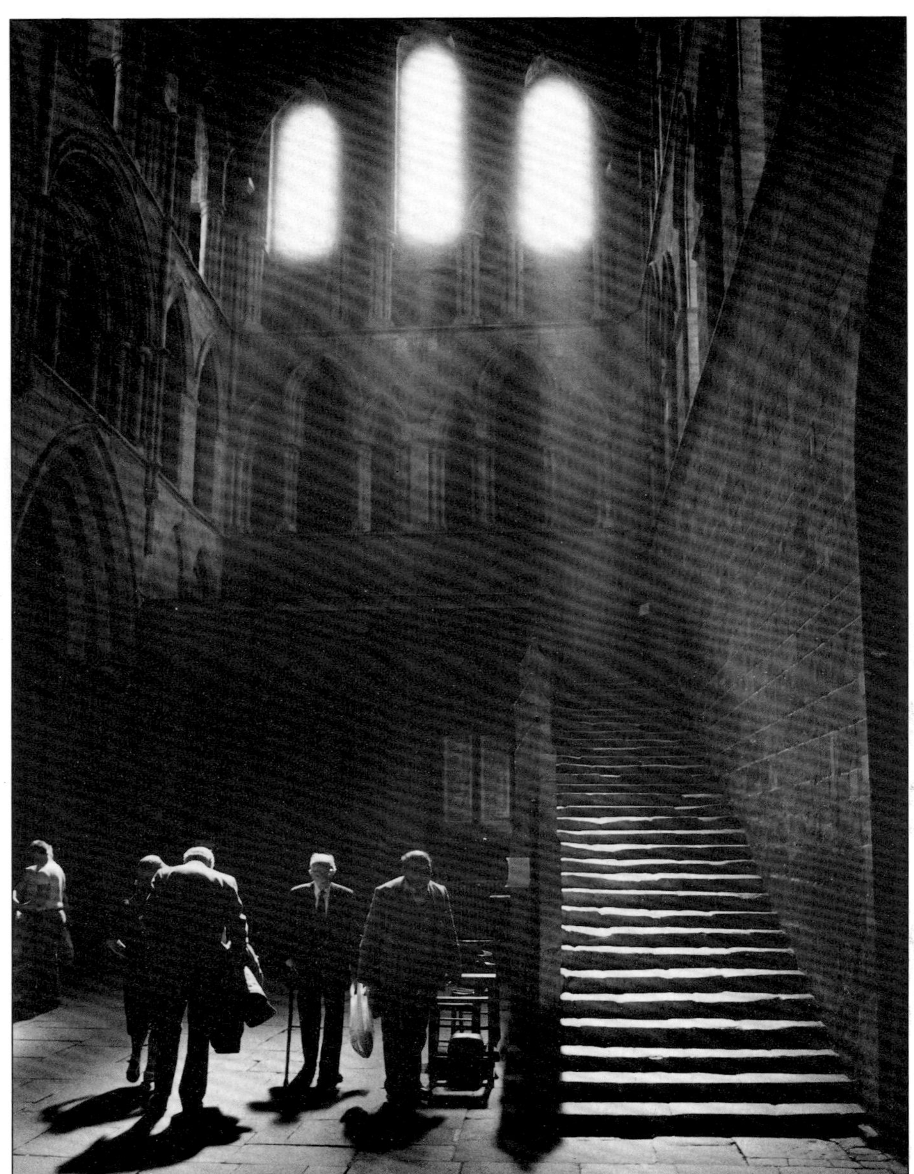

*Hexham Abbey*

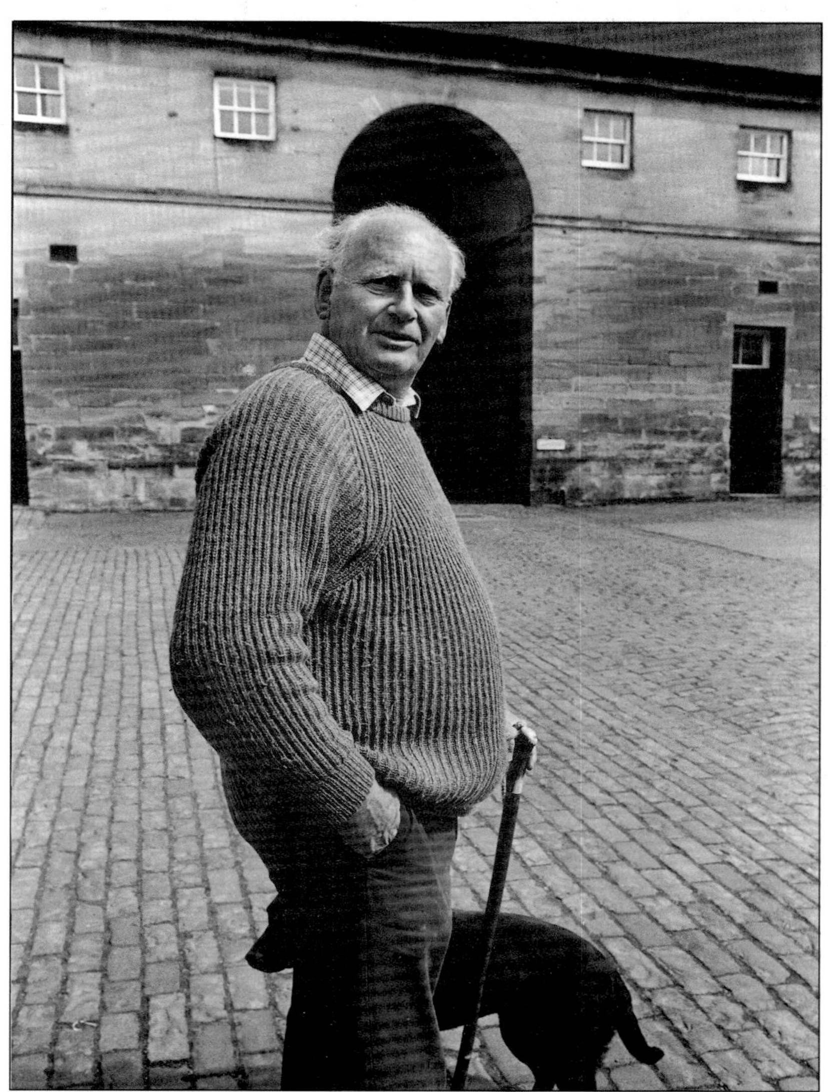

*Viscount Ridley, Northumberland's Lord Lieutenant, of Blagdon Hall*

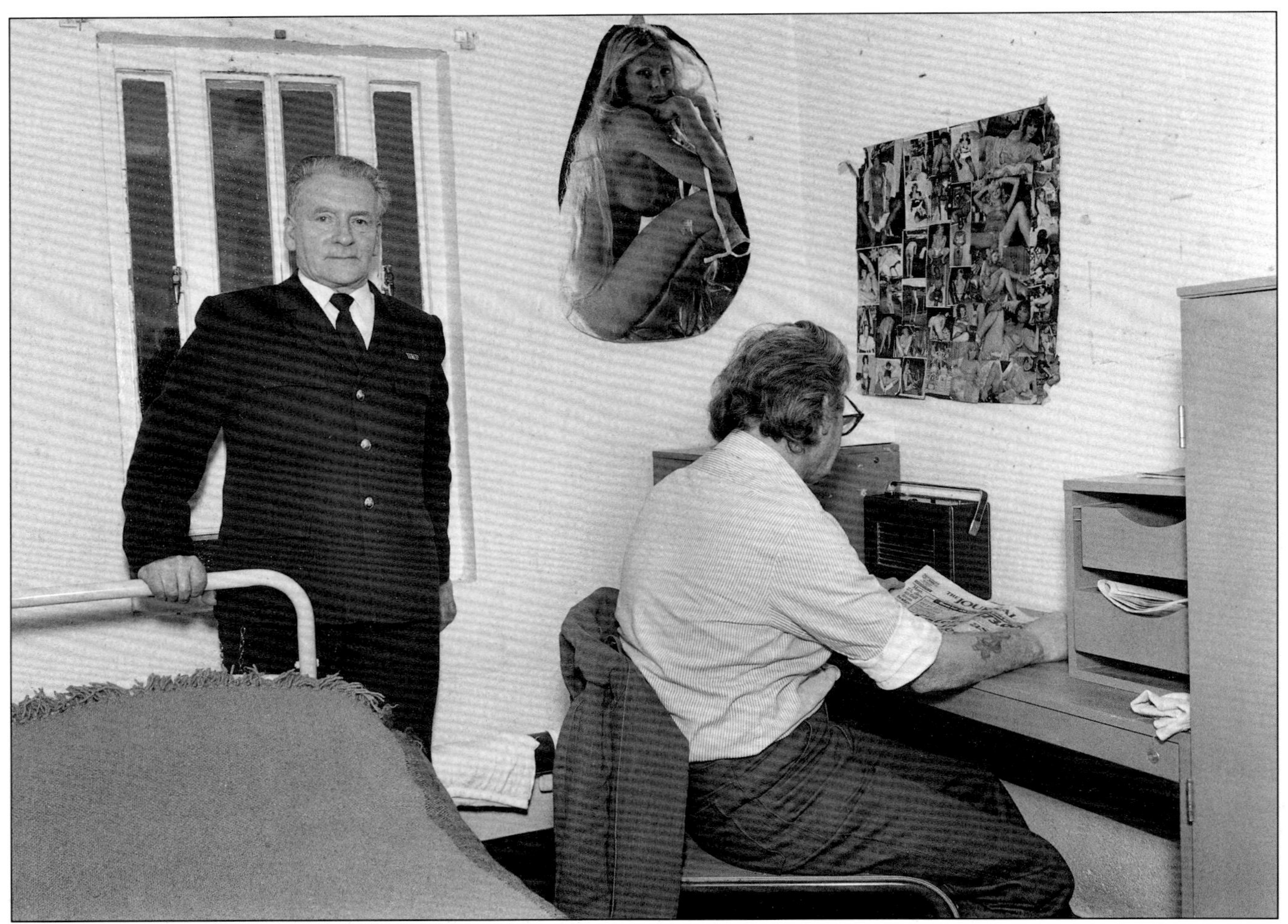

*HM Prison, Acklington*

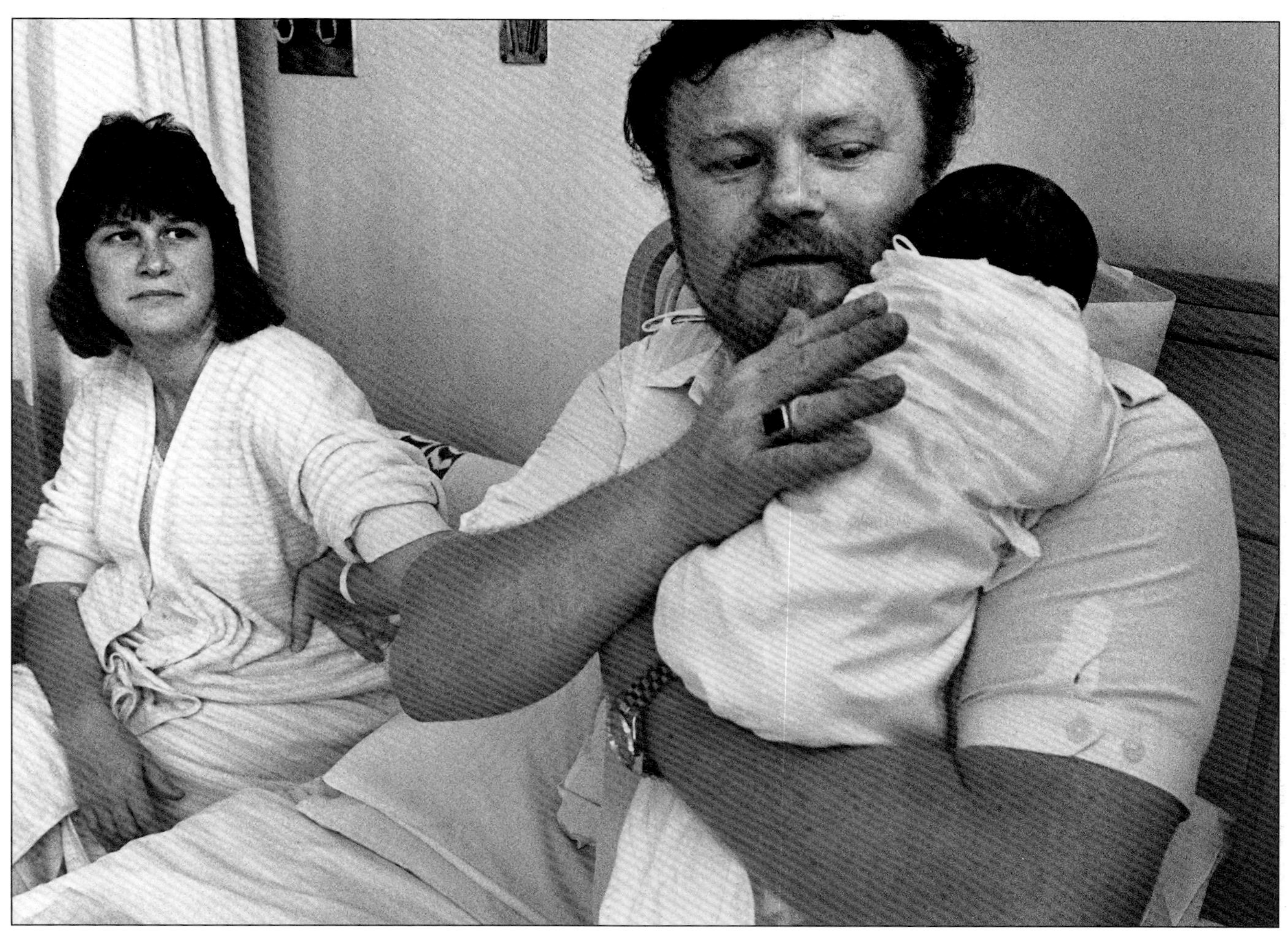

*Maternity ward, Ashington Hospital*

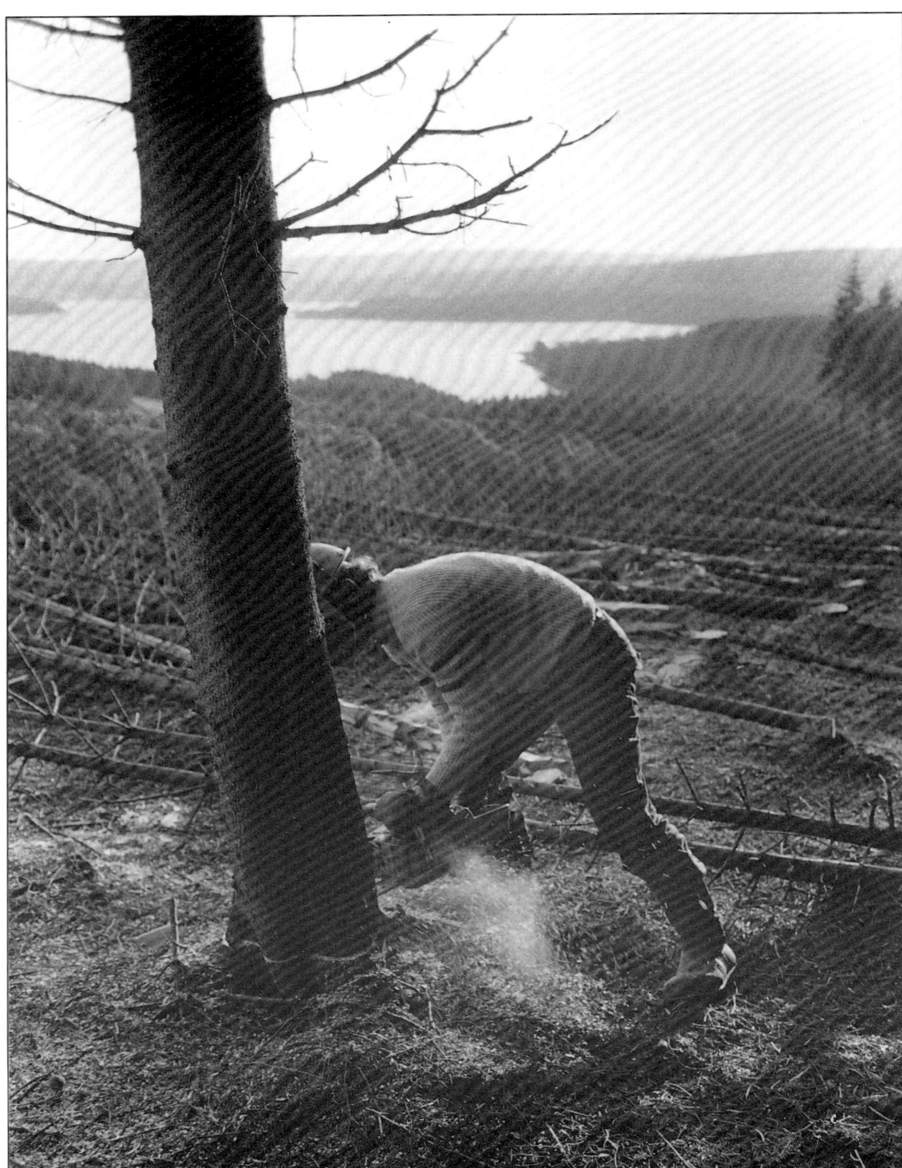

*Kielder Forest*

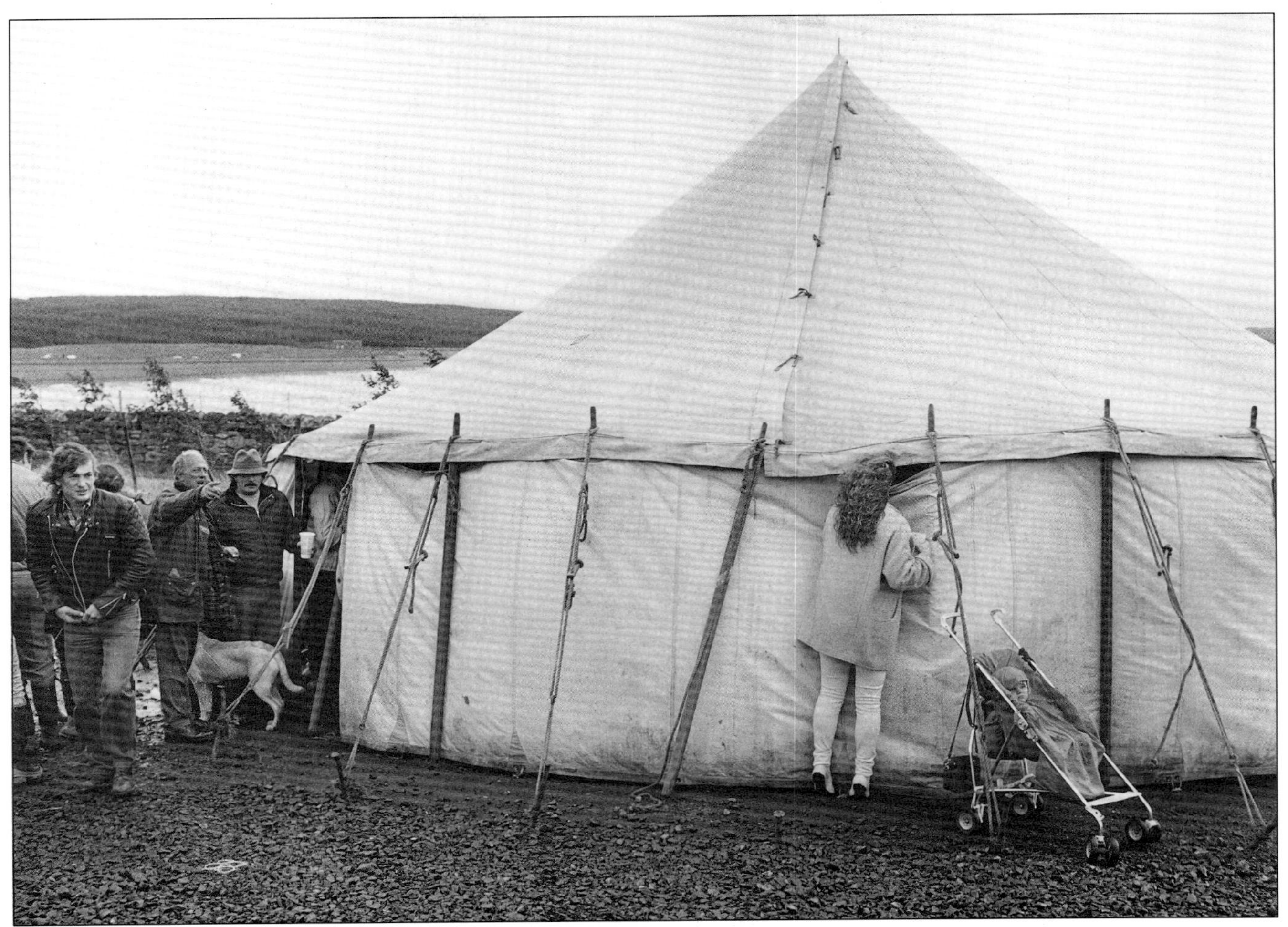

*The beer tent, Falstone Border Shepherds' Show*

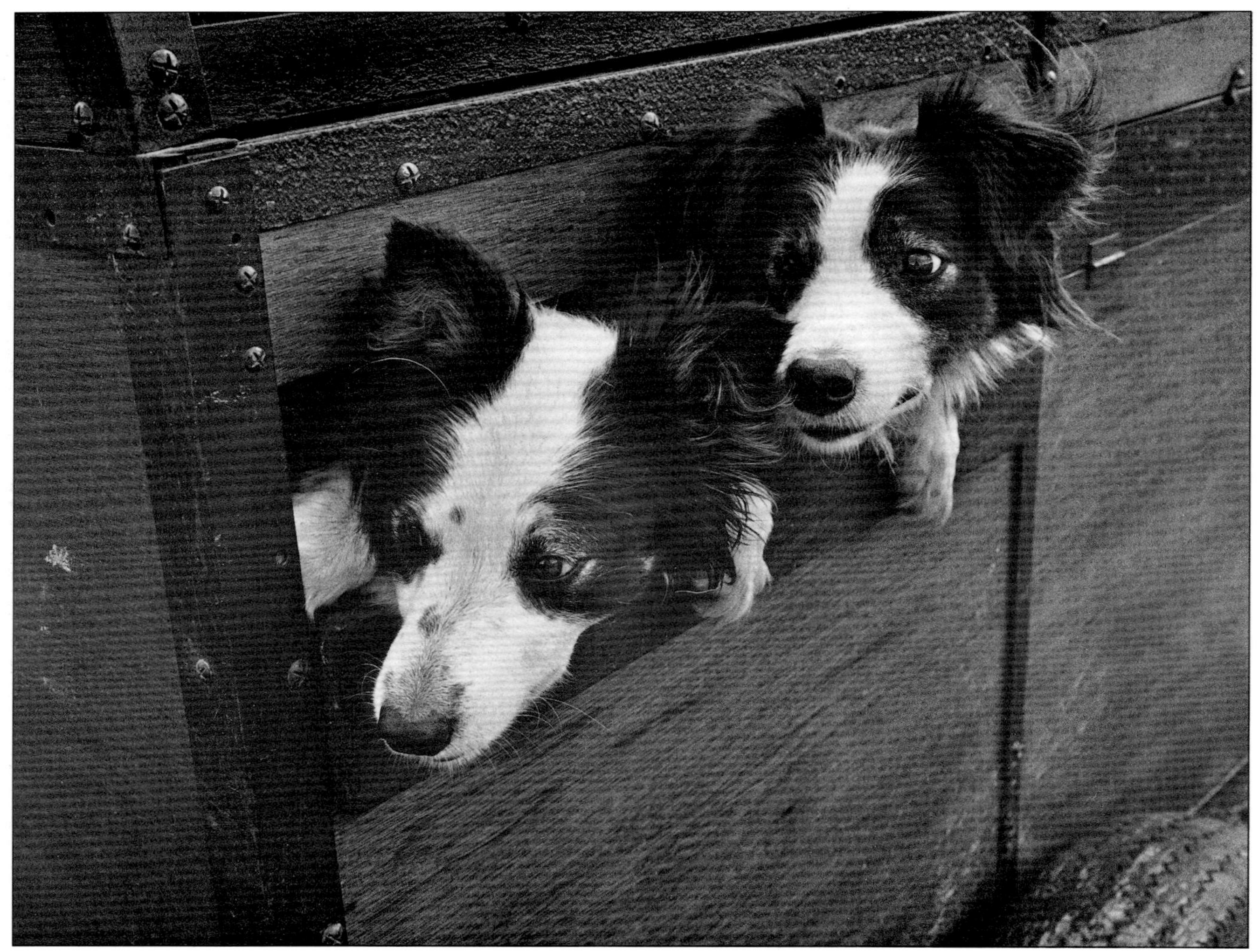

*Border collies*

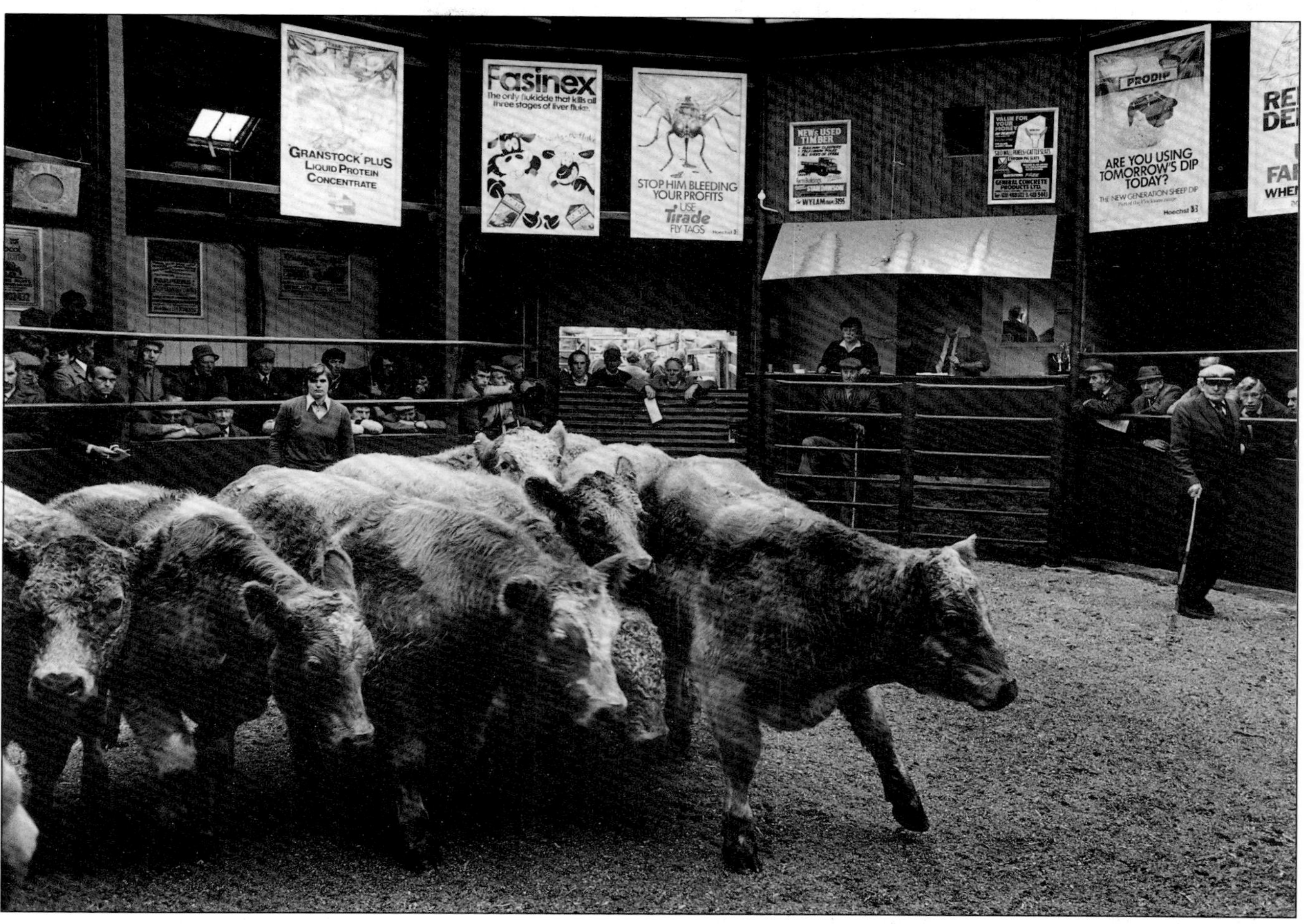


*Scot's Gap auction mart*

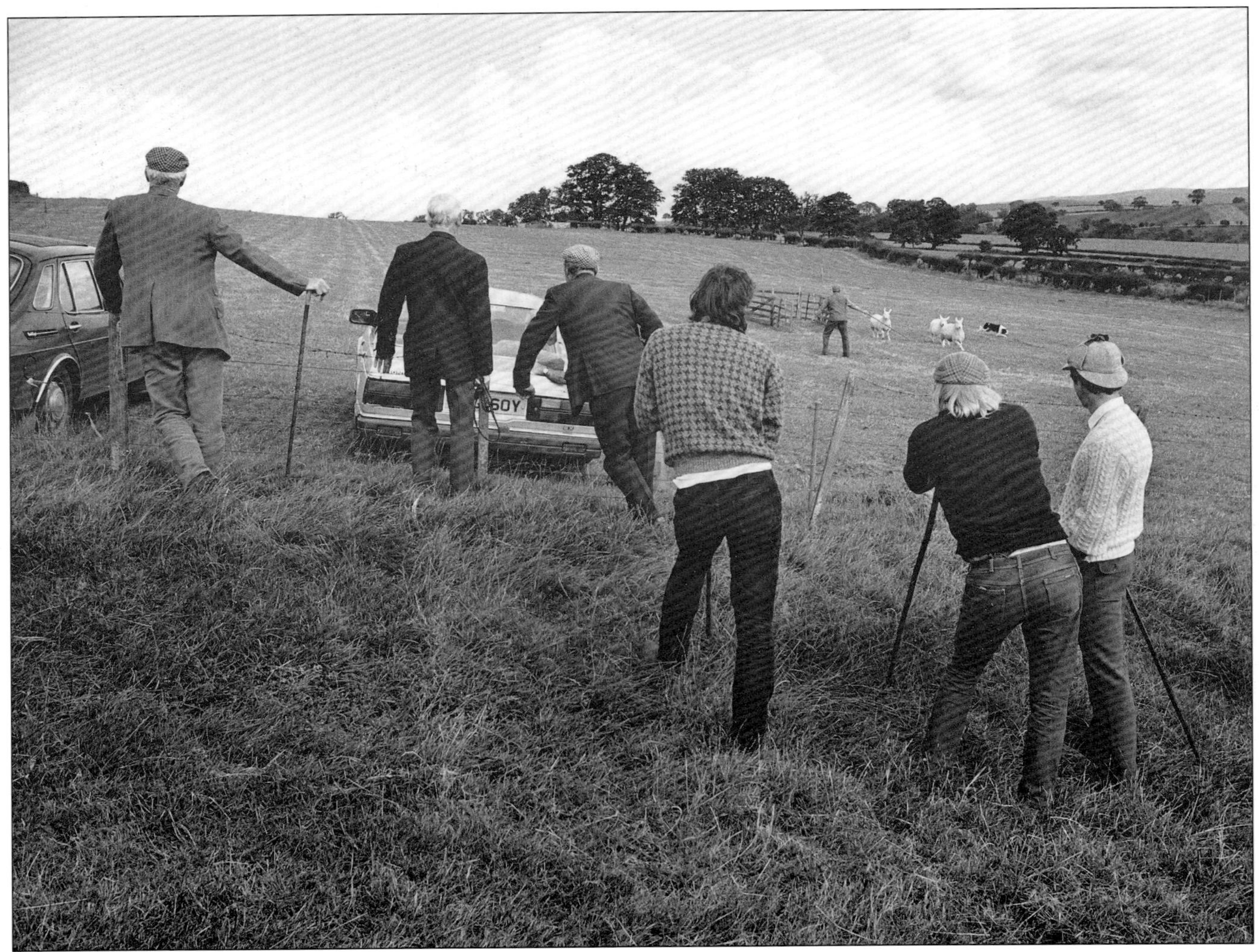

*Sheep dog trials, Ingram Show*

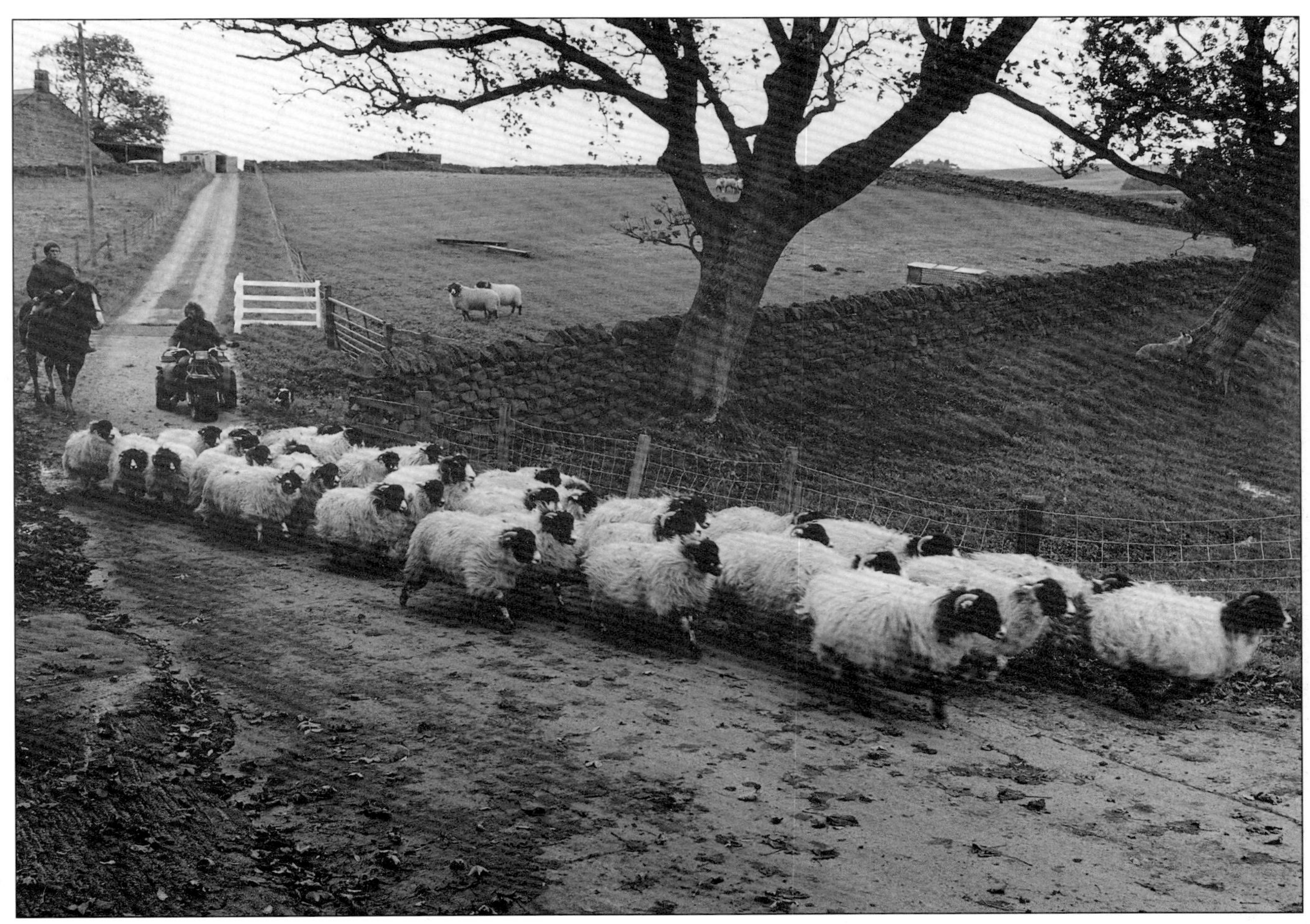

*Blakelaw Farm, near West Woodburn*

*Salmon processors, Tweedmouth*

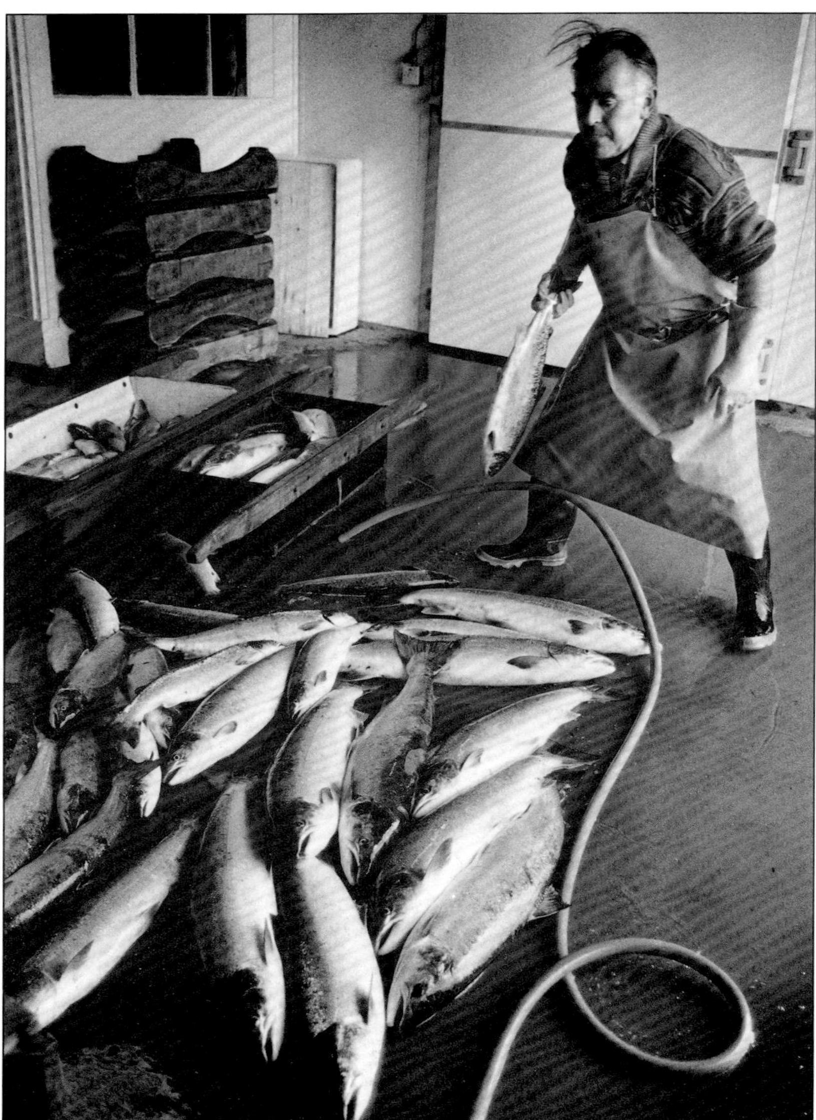

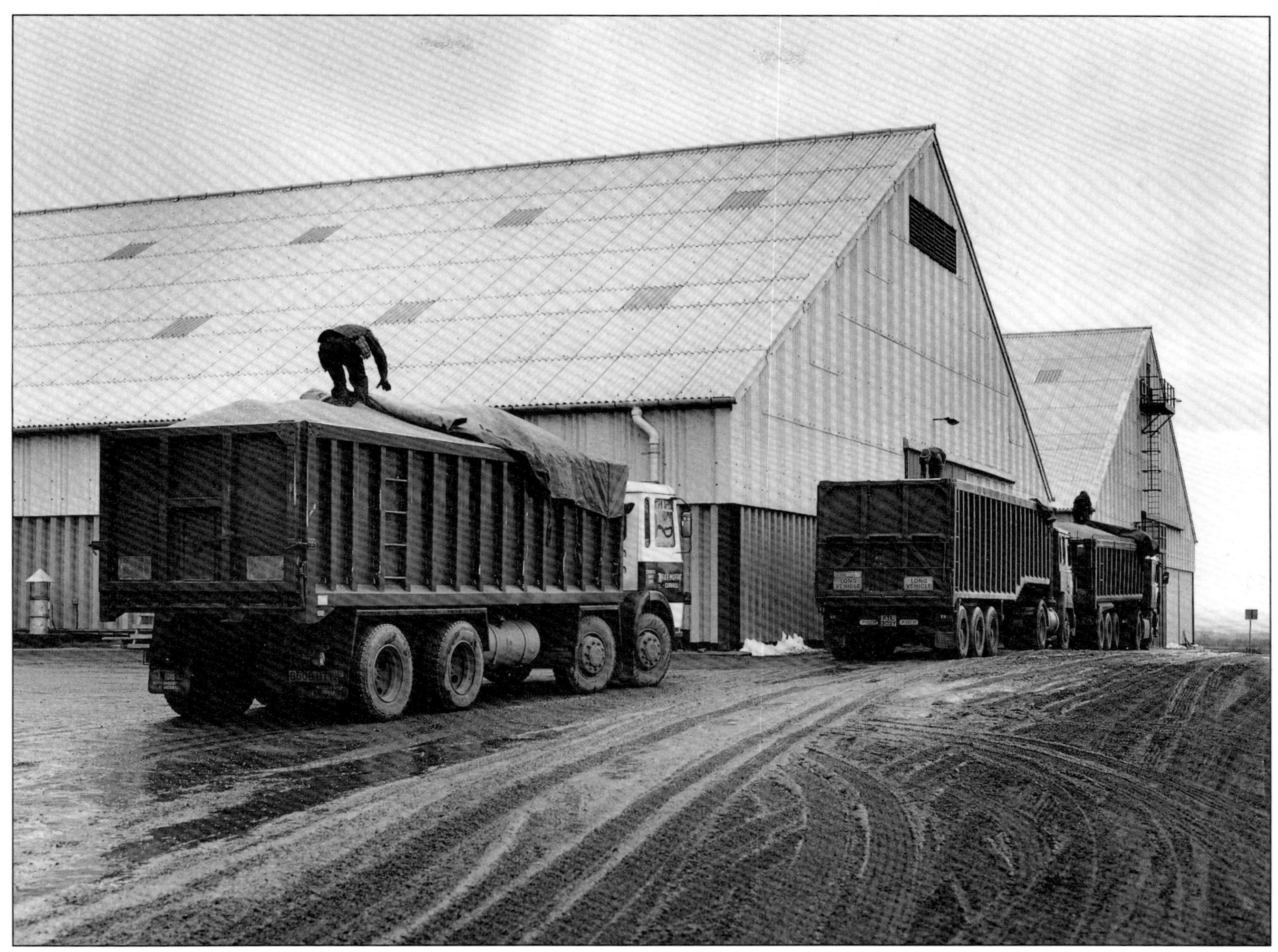

*Lowick grain silo*

ROBSON & COWAN
EVERYTHING
FOR
ESTATE
FARM
ELEY
cartridge dealer
STOCKIST FOR
ICI
ANIMAL
HEALTH
PRODUCTS
DANCE

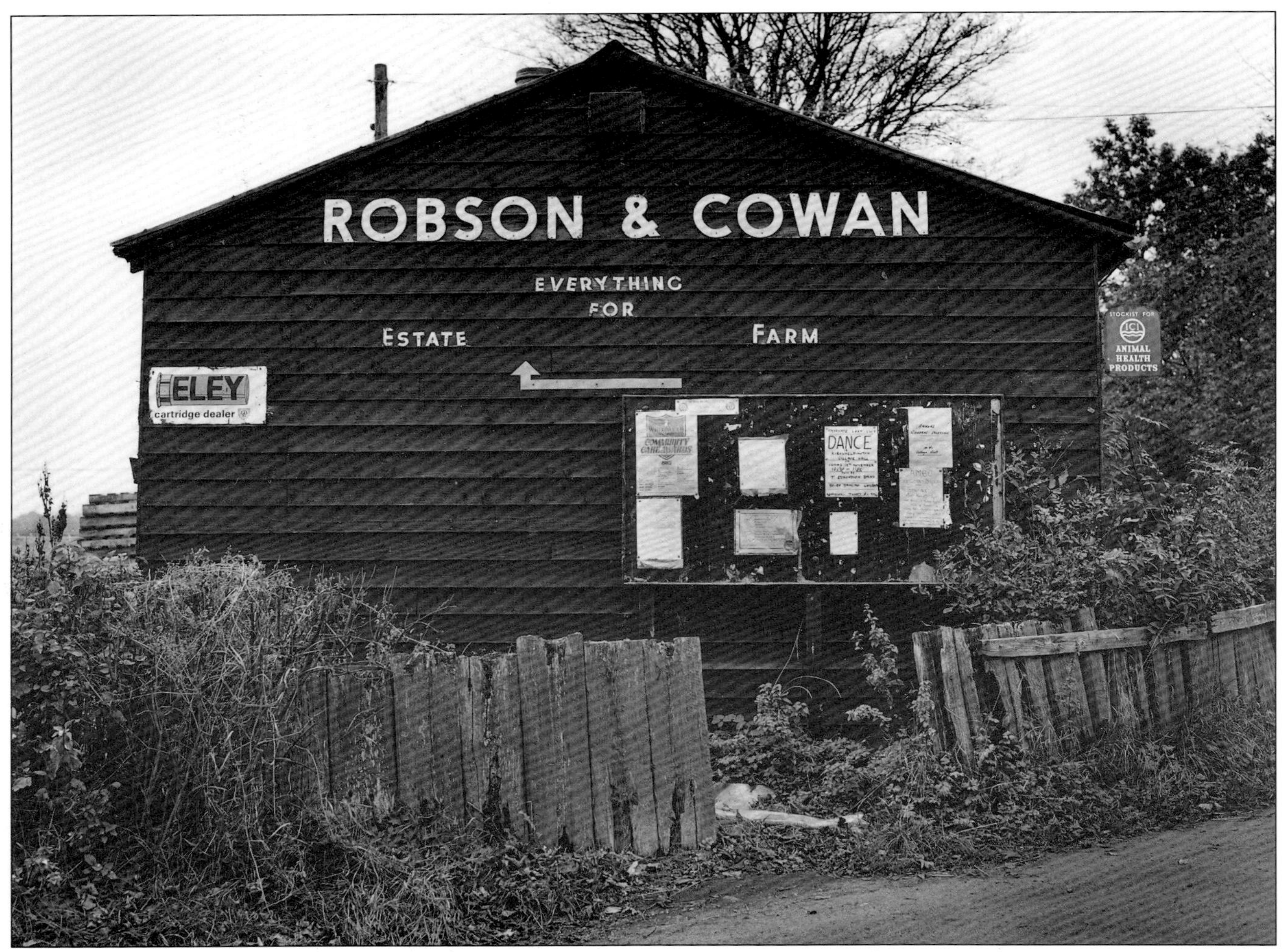

*Scot's Gap*

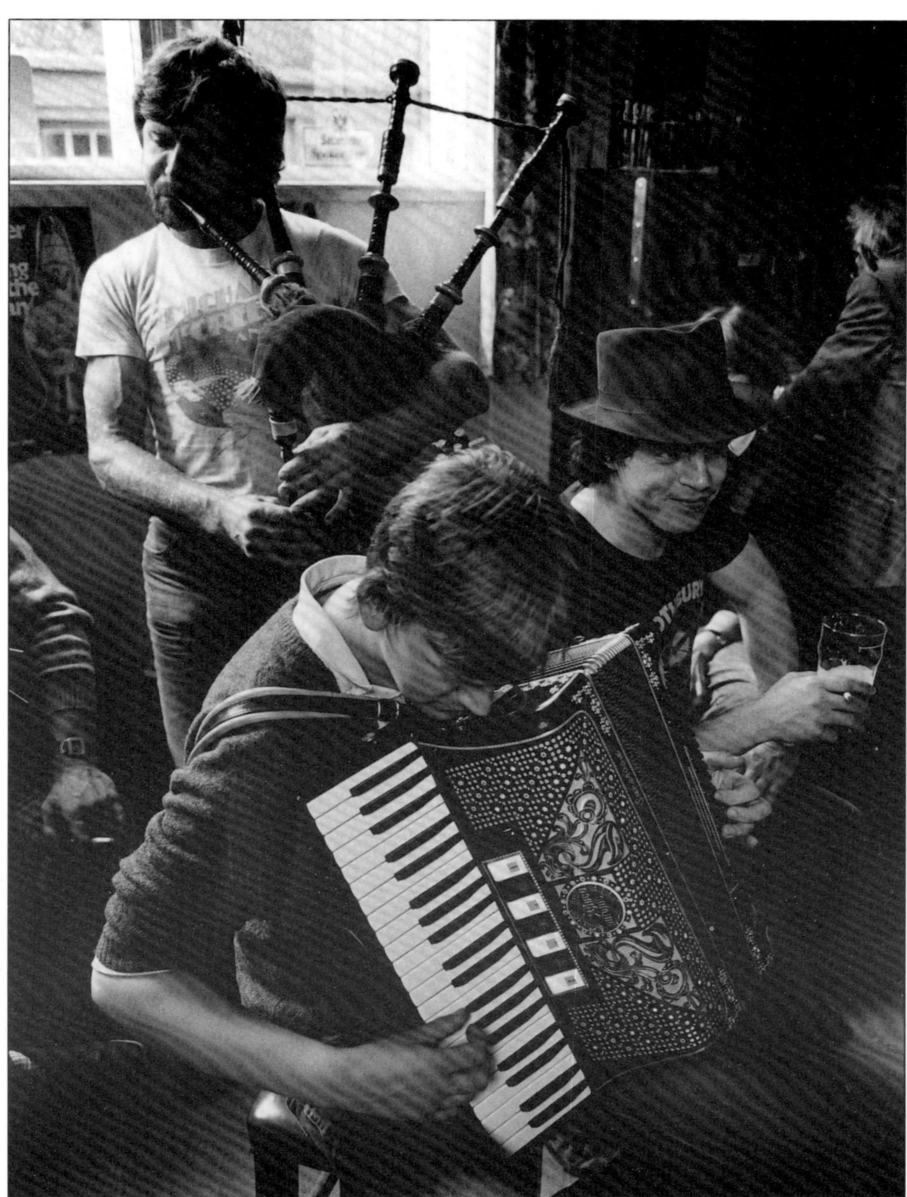

*The Railway Inn, Rothbury, during the Traditional Music Festival*

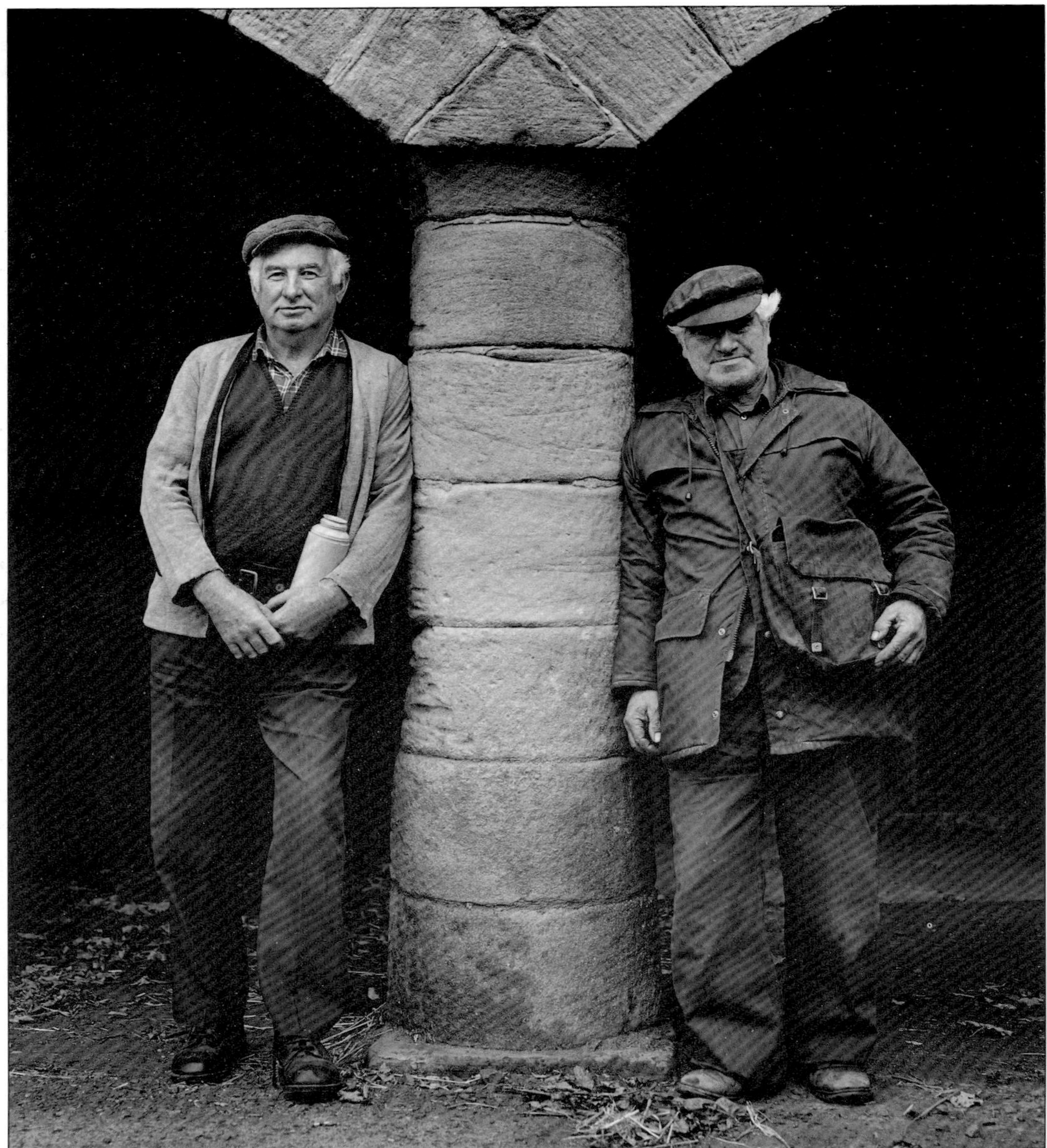

*Farm workers on the Blagdon estate*

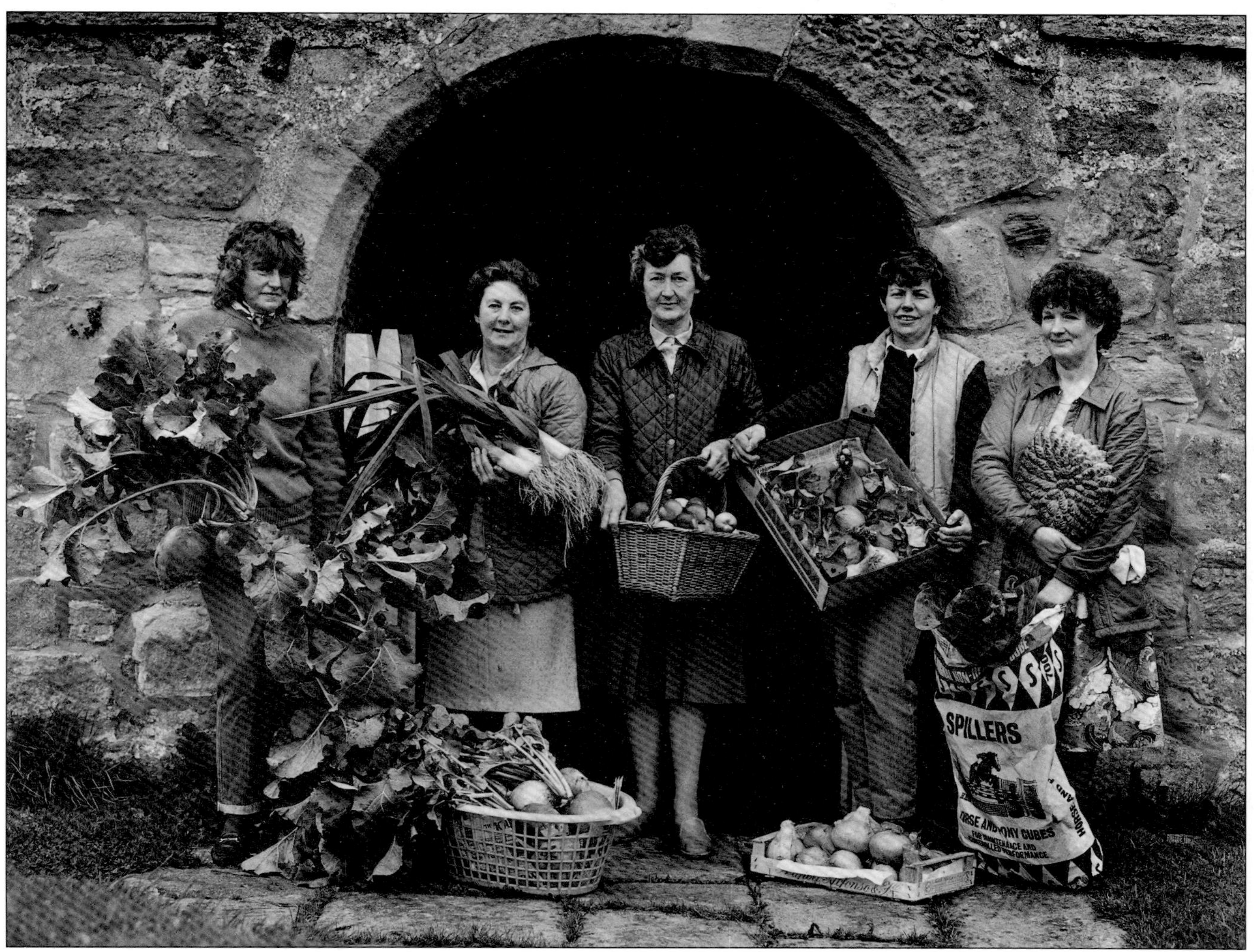


*Harvest Festival preparations about to begin at Kirkwhelpington*

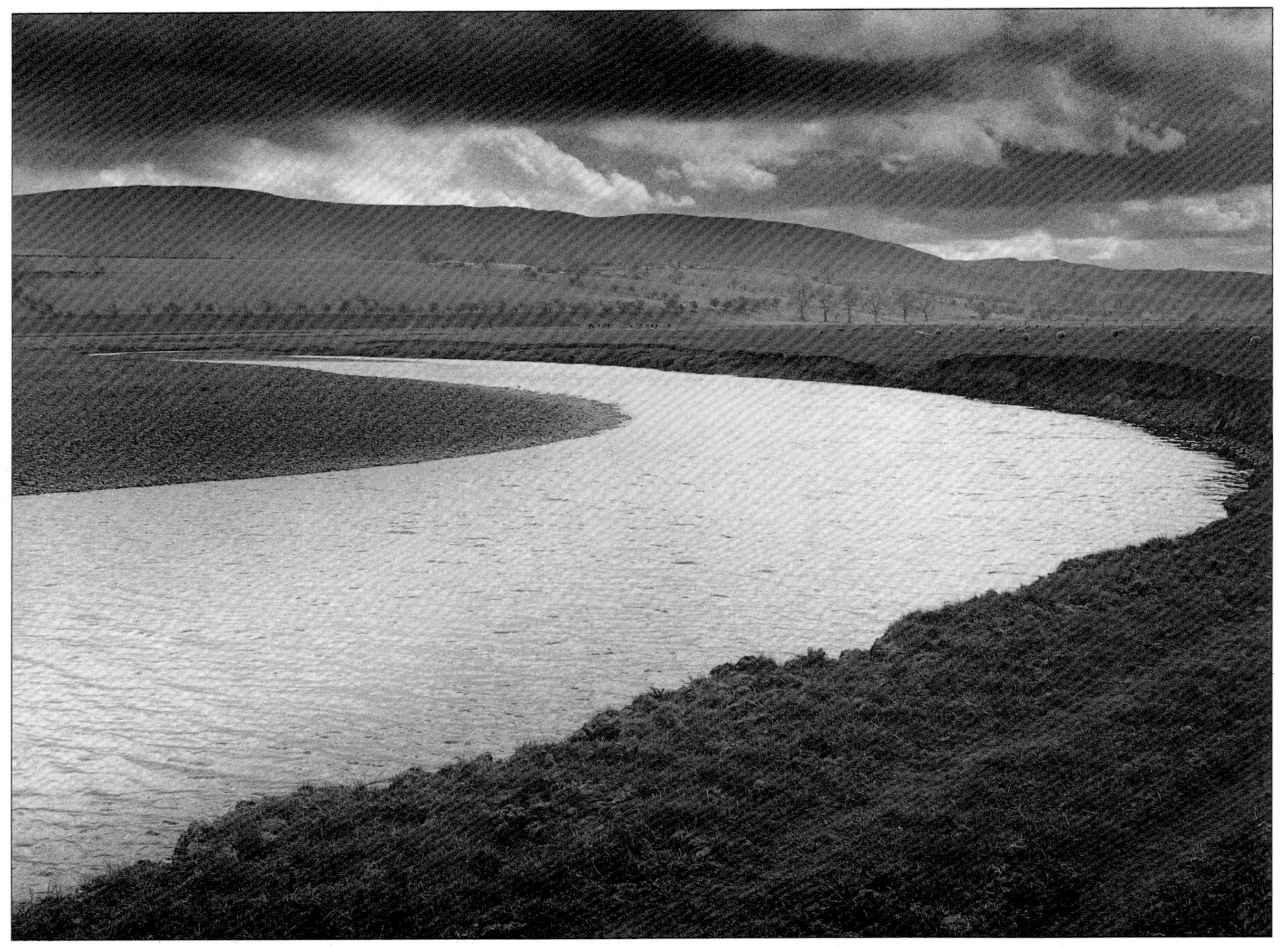

*The River Coquet, near Thropton*

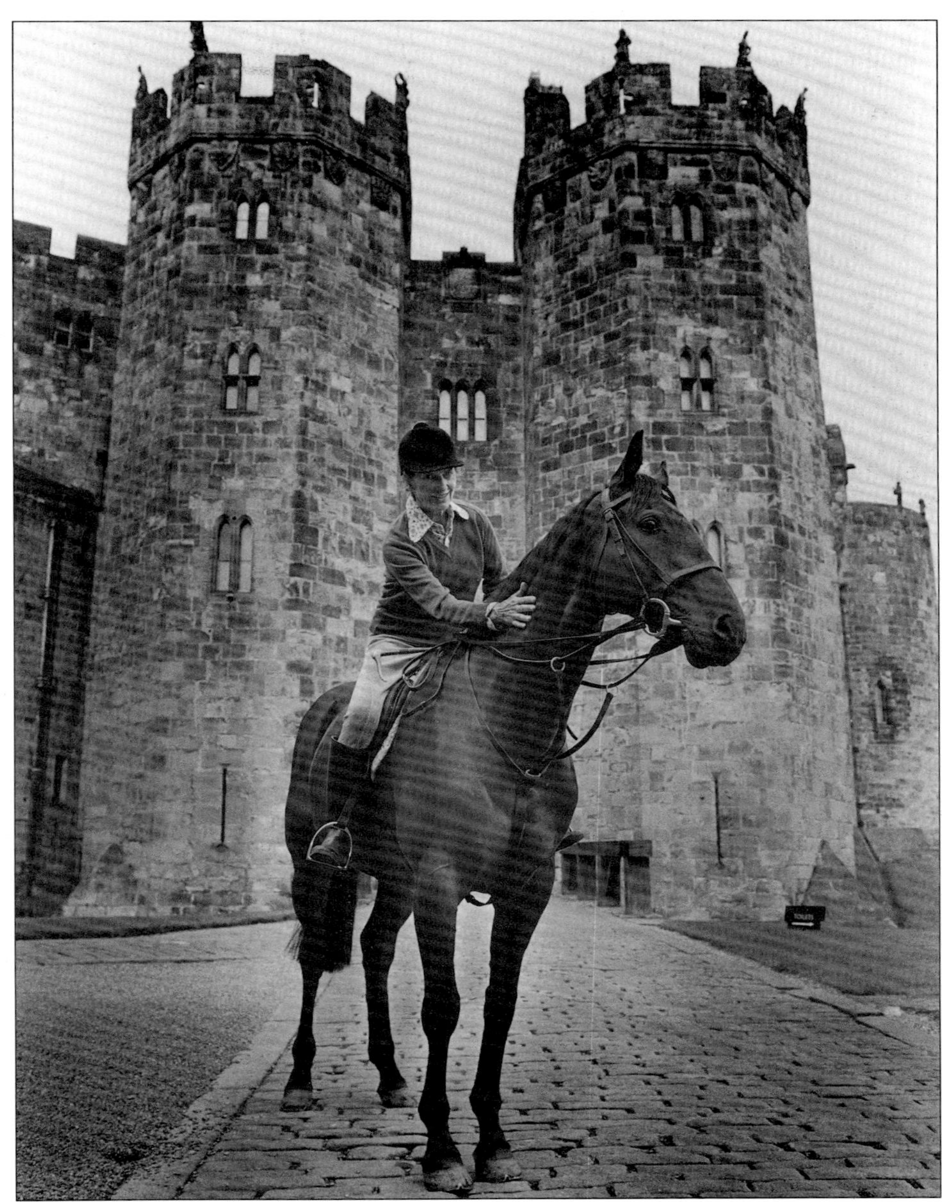

*Her Grace The Duchess of Northumberland, Alnwick Castle*

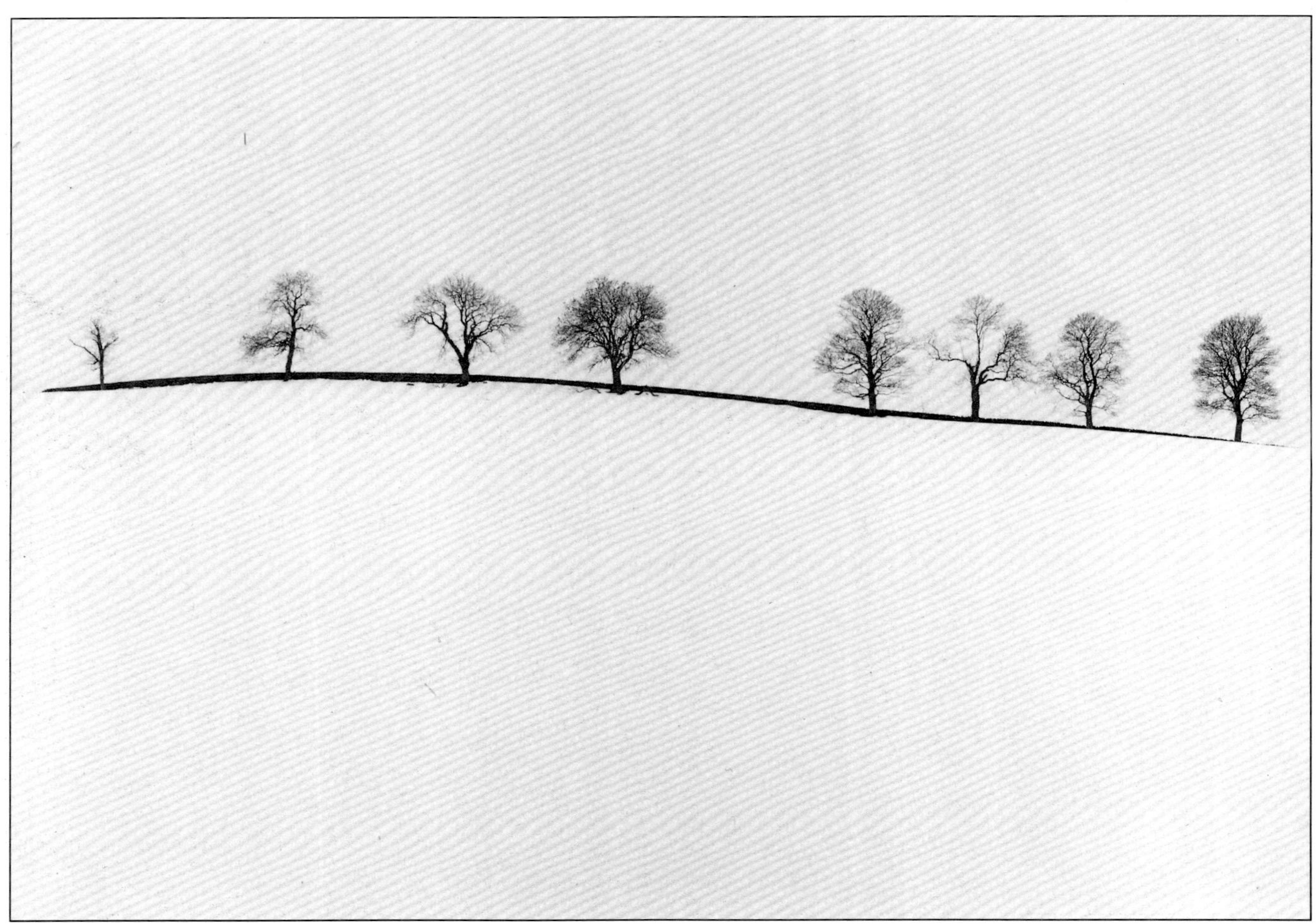

*Near Wallington*

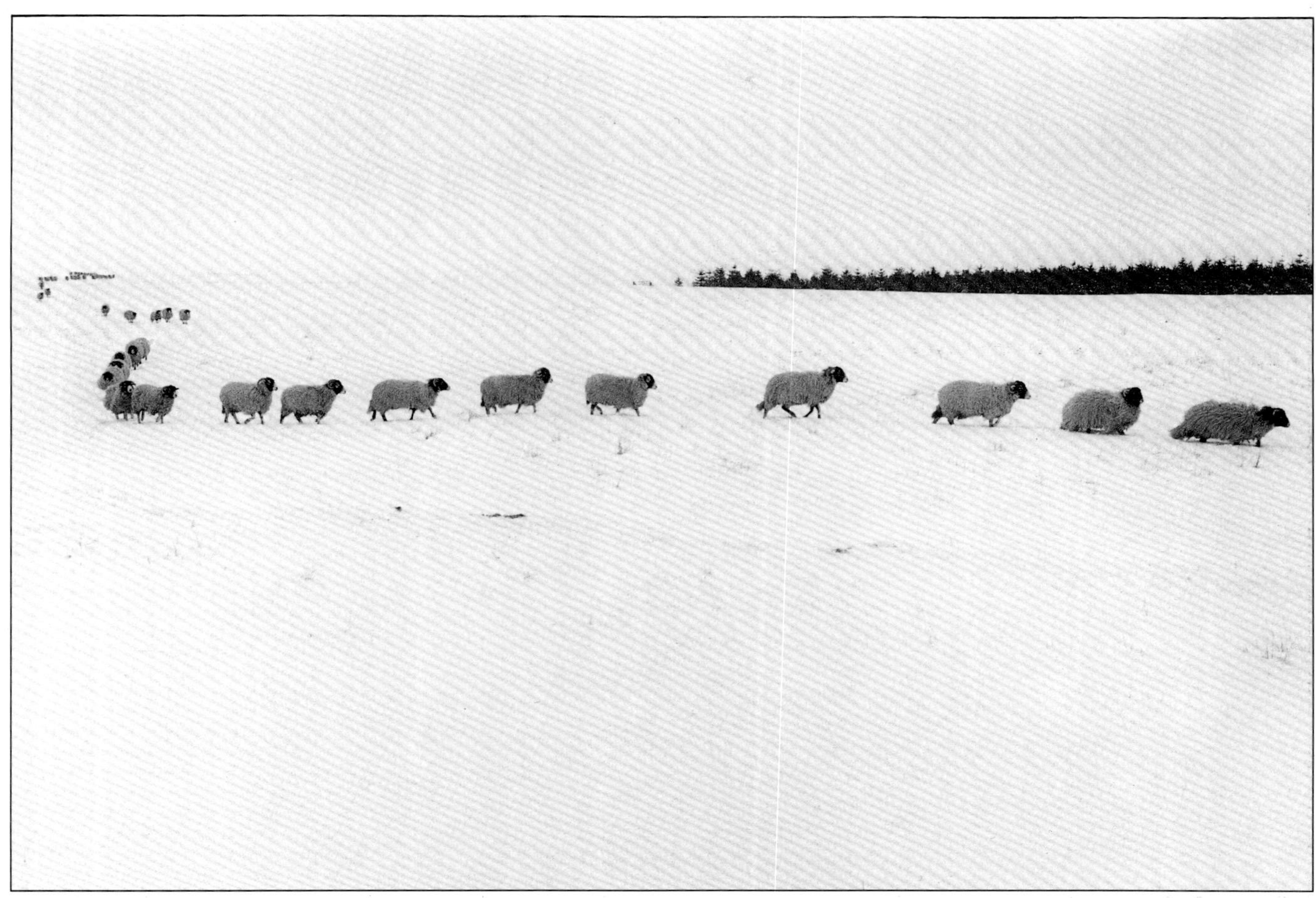

*Ferneyrigg Farm, near Otterburn*

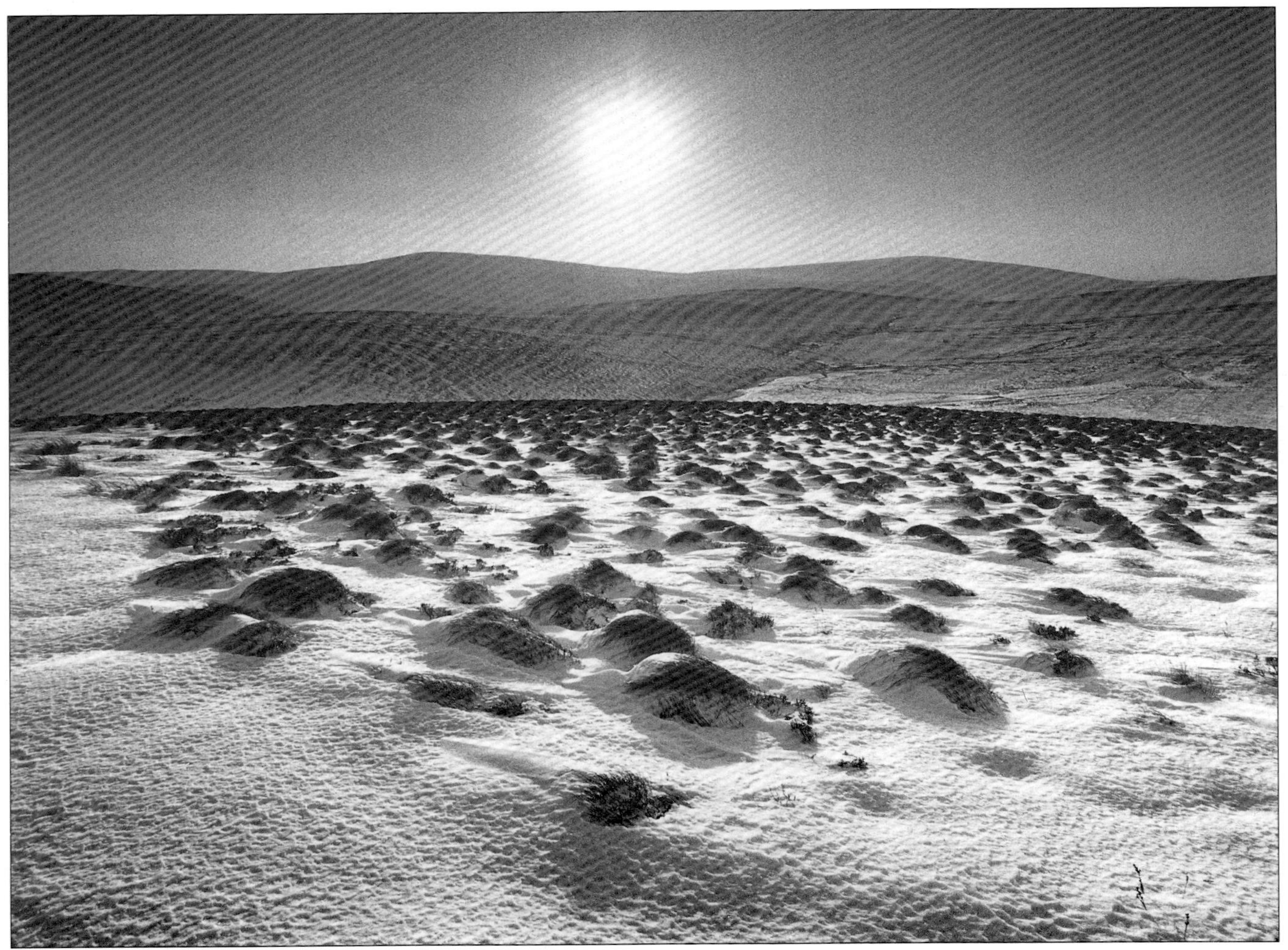

*The Cheviot Hills*

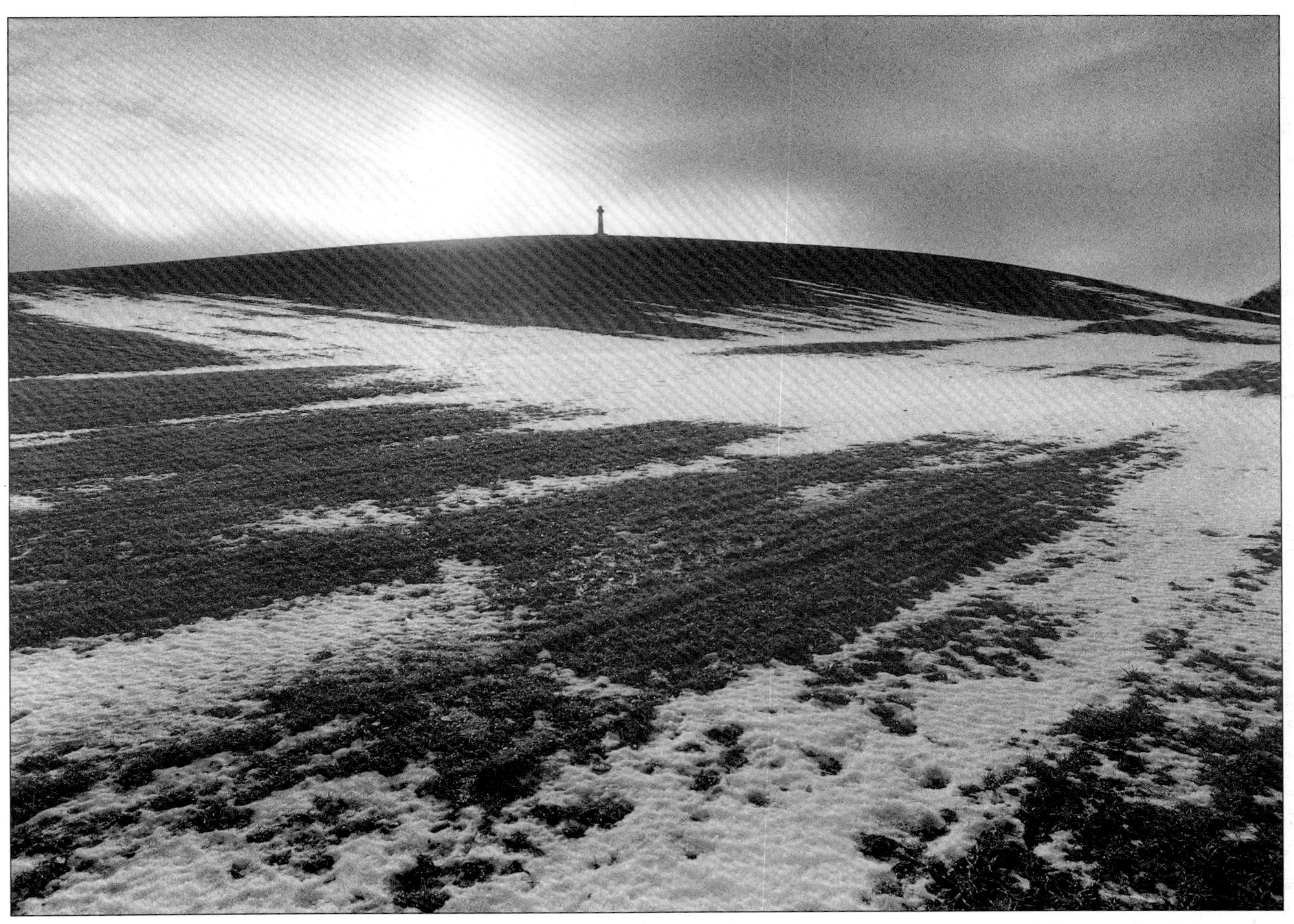

*The site of the Battle of Flodden Field*

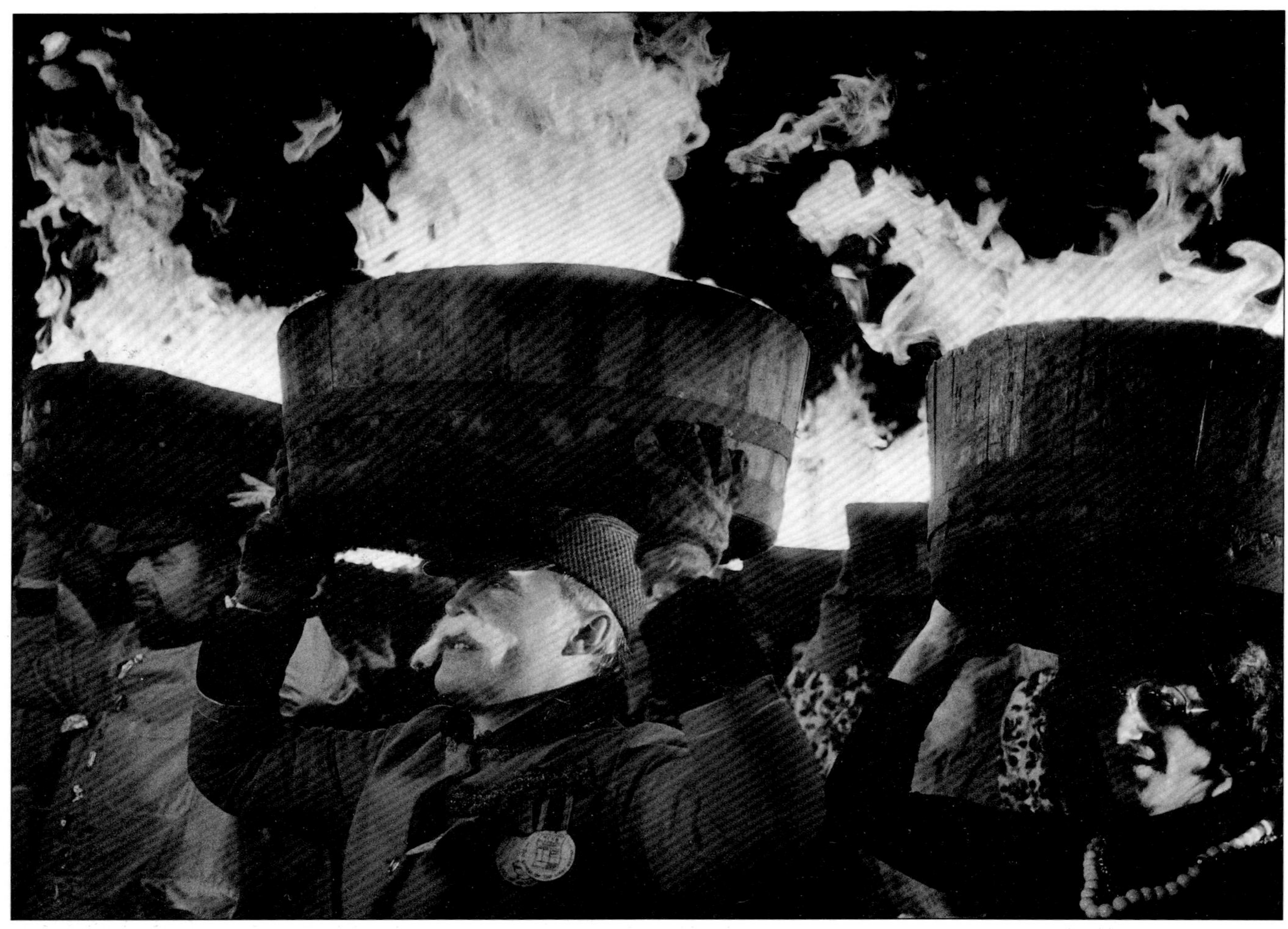

*The new year's eve Fire Festival, Allenheads*

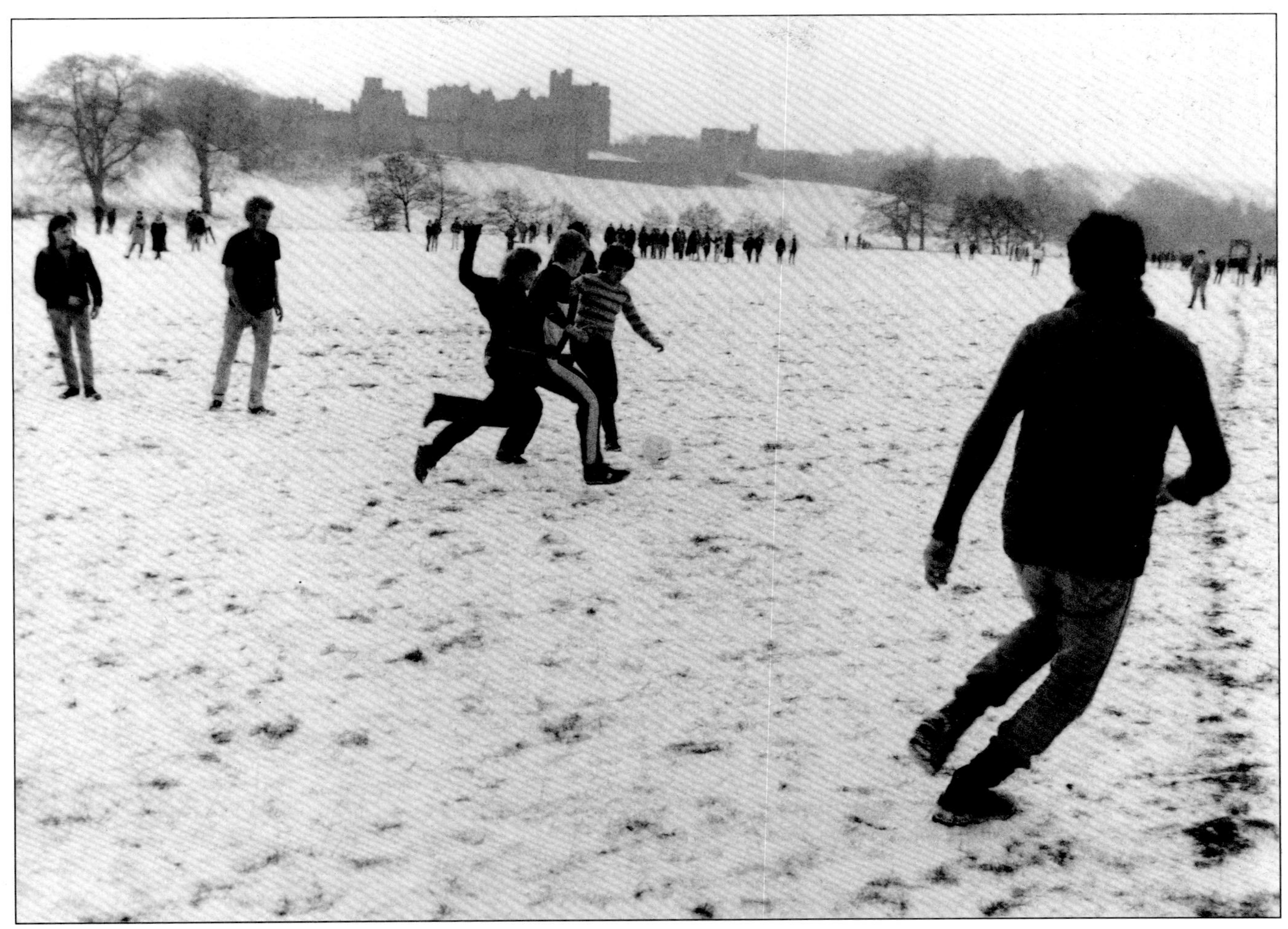

*The Shrove Tuesday football match, near Alnwick*

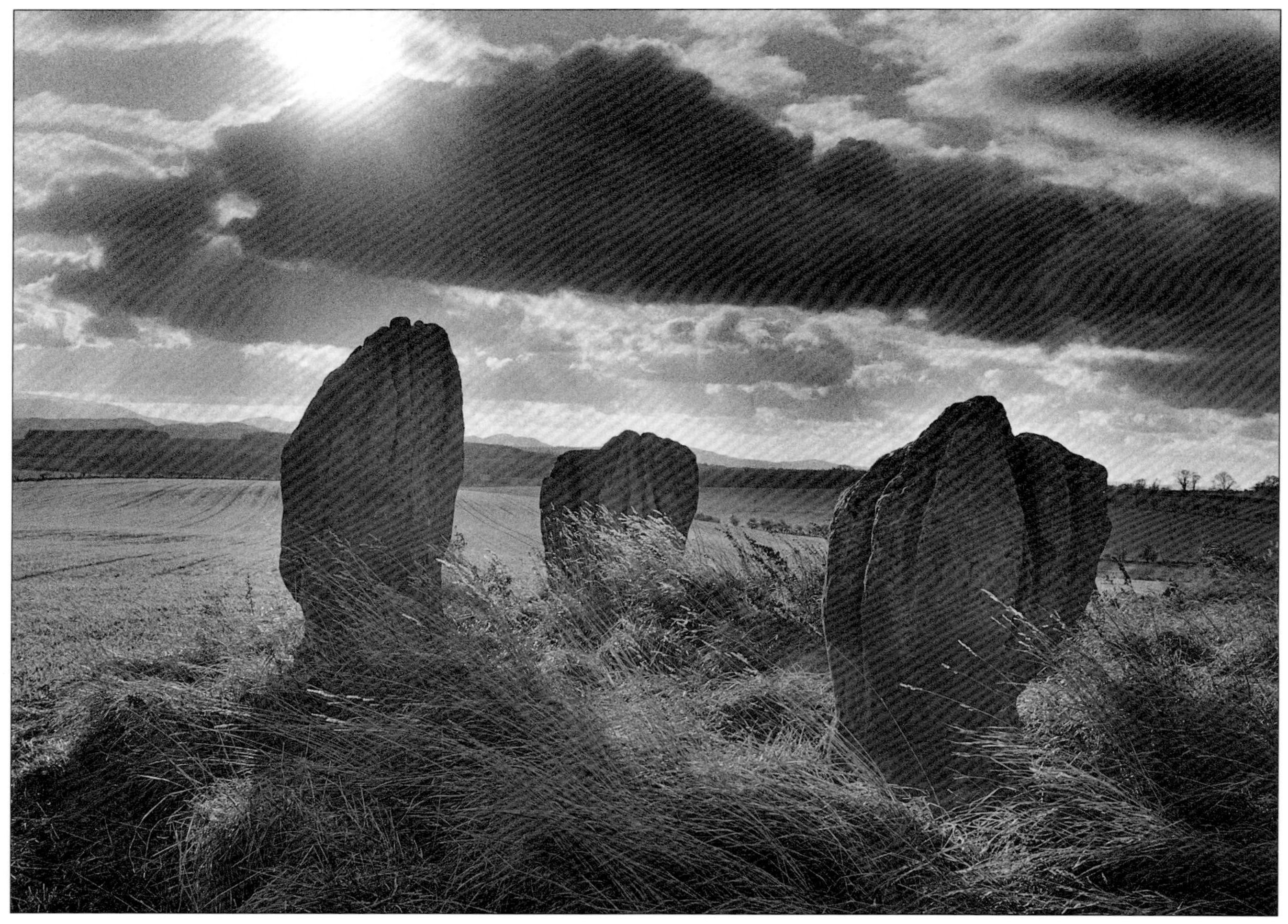

*The prehistoric Duddo Stones, near Wooler*

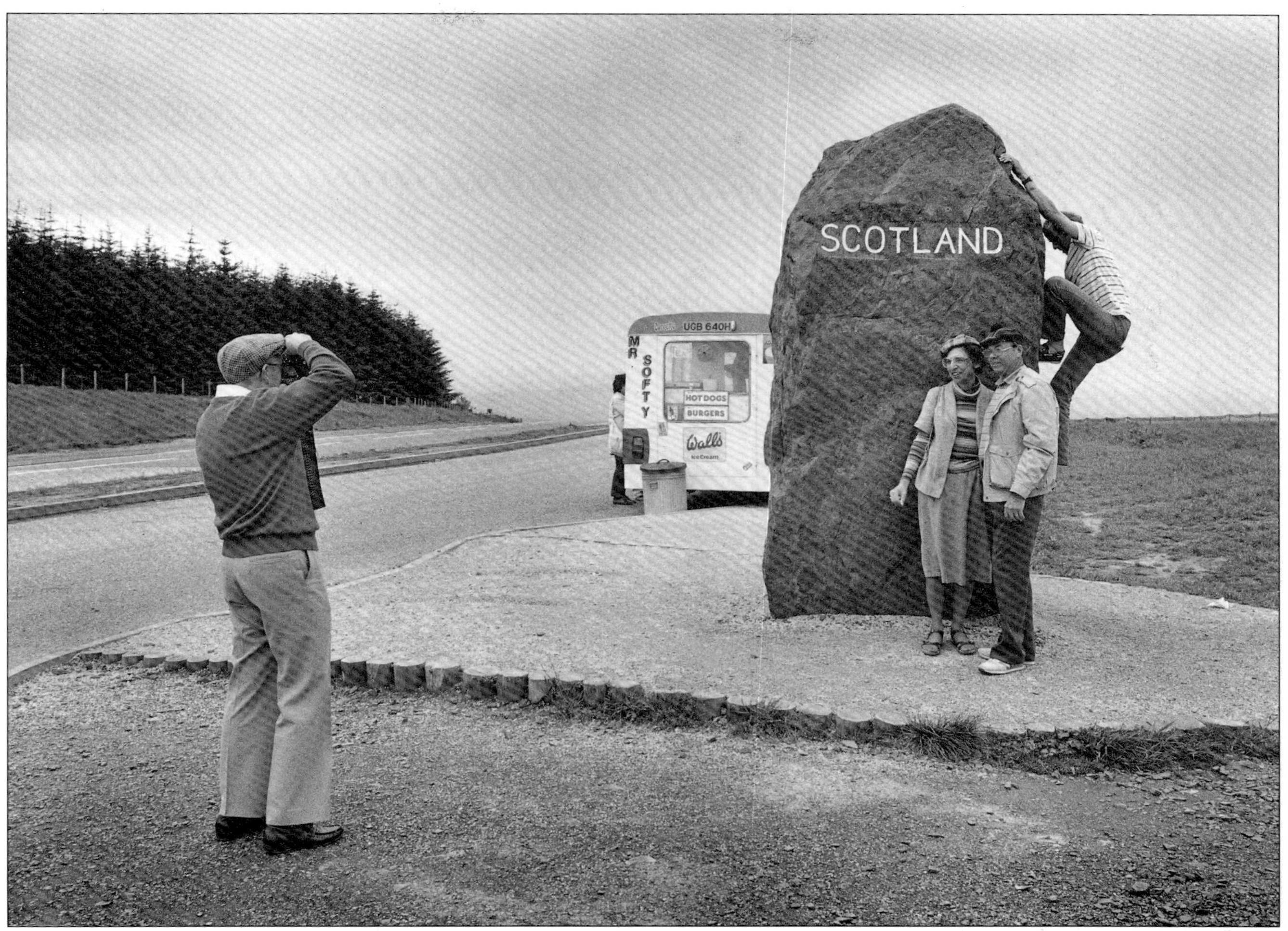


*Tourists at Carter Bar*

*'So seems the life of man, O King, as a sparrow's flight through the hall when you are sitting at meat in winter-tide, the fire on the hearth, the icy rainstorm without.*

*The sparrow flies in at one door and tarries for a moment in the light and heat of the hearth-fire, then flies forth into the darkness whence it came.'*

Words attributed to an elderman of
EDWIN, *King of* NORTHUMBERLAND